Monet at Giverny

Monet at Giverny

Text by Claire Joyes.

Photographic and Editorial research
by Jean-Marie Toulgouat and Robert Gordon.

With a commentary on the paintings at Giverny,
by Andrew Forge.

Mathews Miller Dunbar · London 1975

Book design and typography by Peter Dunbar and Roy Walker, M.S.I.A.

Text copyright © 1975 by Claire Joyes.
Text copyright © 1975 by Andrew Forge.

Originally produced and published in 1975 by Mathews Miller Dunbar Ltd.,
51 Endell Street, London WC2H 9AJ, England.

Printed by CTD, Twickenham, England.

ISBN 0 903811 15 4

The authors would like to thank especially James Butler, Monsieur Charles Durand-Ruel, Monsieur Gruet for his advice on the Durand-Ruel archives, Madame Simone Salerou-Piguet, Marc and Philippe Piguet, Monsieur Le Flour of the Truffaut archives, Monsieur Fuchs, Monsieur Jacques Carlu, Monsieur Richebé, Madame Marguerite Lavenu, Monsieur Jean Francois Lavenu, Monsieur Le Gal and Monsieur Lecointe. two of the surviving gardeners who worked at Giverny during Monet's lifetime, Madame Verneiges, Monsieur Sirot and John Rewald. They would particularly like to acknowledge the help and guidance provided by Peter Dunbar in all stages of the preparation of this book.

Contents

Publisher's Note

Claire Joyes and Jean-Marie Toulgouat live and work in Giverny. Jean-Marie Toulgouat's childhood was spent in the Monet household. His own recollections, and those of many other people who have been interviewed provide a description of Monet's domestic and horticultural interest during his life at Giverny. A life of strict ritual, of discipline in his work and a passion for his garden are described in the following personal account given by Claire Joyes. Robert Gordon and Jean-Marie Toulgouat's interviews with the two gardeners who are still living, with Monet's cook and with Jim Butler, give us a new and revealing insight into Monet's way of life based on personal recollections.

Jim Butler was Mme Monet's grandson who lived and grew up in the Monet household. His accounts of his life with Monet constitute a considerable part of the following impressions, and his reconstruction of the garden (see plan, pages 34–35) is based on his expertise as a botanist and his knowledge of the garden during Monet's lifetime. This account of Monet's domestic life is based on facts attested to in private diaries, taped interviews and the statements of Monet's relatives. They evoke the moods and events at Giverny in Monet's time and provide a descriptive and tender personal view. They show how the rituals, delights and vicissitudes of the Monet household establish a base and a support for the painter and the work he did at Giverny.

Monet at Giverny

Andrew Forge

When Monet finally bought his property at Giverny in 1890 he was fifty years old. His reputation was firmly established, his work sought after and the anxieties and privations of the first half of his working life were over. He was at a stage where many smaller artists would have begun to relax the tension in their work and would have accepted, perhaps, that their styles were formed and their researches over. But with him the opposite was true. The restless energy that had carried him forward in the past and had allowed him to paint the carefree, scintillating subjects of the 'sixties and 'seventies even while he was pursued by creditors or by anxieties for the well-being of his family, had not in the slightest abated.

Nor had his intentions changed. The general direction was the same as it had always been, ever since, at the age of eighteen, he had been persuaded by Boudin to work directly from nature. The project was simply to take the appearances of nature as the material for art.

This did not in itself imply a new way to work. Ever since the early years of the century, academic painters in France had been giving increasing attention to landscape as one among the categories of High Art. It was taken for granted that sketching directly out of doors was an essential practice of landscape painters. These sketches *(ébauches)* were highly valued. The idea was that the artist's originality would be most clearly revealed through the effort to capture his direct impressions at top speed. The concepts of spontaneity and originality came to be closely linked: one became the condition for the other. But—and this is the important point—these studies made directly in the open air were not in any way to be confused with the painter's real work, with what he presented to the public. This could only be taken seriously if it was 'finished', and it could only be finished if it had passed through a period of gestation in which the raw data and the 'inspiration' of the sketch was reshaped and organised by the painter's knowledge and sense of style.

What was truly radical about the small number of painters with whom Monet came to identify himself—Boudin, Daubigny, Jonkind—was the determination to instate the sketch as the final work. This was not only a challenge to the mass public which was totally unused to seeing anything but the highly finished and elaborate public works on the walls of the Salon, but also to the rest of the painting profession who saw the secrets of the studio being exposed and the validity of their skills challenged.

Once Monet had started to work from observation, his commitment to the approach was complete. There is no transition in his work from a traditional to a plein airiste position. As soon as he begins to paint nature on the spot he accepts that the real world is the source both of subject-matter and style—that is to say, the 'how' as well as the 'what'. The implications of this position prove to be more complicated and more demanding with each year of his working life.

What was demanded, as time went on, was that he should ask himself not only what he saw but how he saw. But to answer these questions is not just a matter of using one's eyes attentively. It is also to question the way that previous experience shapes one's expectations. For a painter, this means above all to question one's *pictorial* expectations and to be able to see the way in which the culture of pictures filters or moulds the visible world. Seeing is a mental process akin to thought: the attempt really to 'see' oneself 'seeing' is as virtiginous an undertaking as to 'think' oneself 'thinking', and as soon as Monet embarked upon it he found that he had not only to free himself from learned ways of drawing, the traditional constructions of the studio, but also to be revising and continually checking his own methods and the way they in turn were shaping the way that he saw.

The link between what he painted and how he painted was a living one. He could never afford familiarity and he had to be continually challenging himself and his eye with new places and new conditions; and the challenge extended equally to his own marks—brush strokes, palette, the look of the canvas.

Monet's generation as a whole had renounced traditional subject-matter—the attitude that the subject of the painting must be somehow exemplary, must convey general values drawn from the past and enacted through allegory or anecdote. For the impressionist it was the 'real' world that counted—and what was real was what could be seen. Any impressionist painting has a certain quality of objectivity and an absence of *parti pris*, at least on the descriptive level, which seems to separate it from any earlier painting. It is a quality which we might call photographic if it were not for the aesthetic selectivity manifest in impressionist brushwork and colour. This begs all sorts of questions, for example why 'see' only what is painless, sunny, bourgeois? One way of describing impressionist 'reality' or descriptive level would be to say that it avoids strong emotion. Even so, certain of the impressionist generation evince a more specific view of human affairs than others. A Pissarro landscape has something to tell us about human life and the human meaning of the seasons. If there are figures in a Renoir they will relate to each other and will express a human state. In Monet, on the other hand, figures are just figures, lumps of dark suits or flowery dresses among other lumps that take the light. A figure walking down a road will read as a dark accent, an abrupt conjunction of brush strokes, nothing more. After the mid-eighties it is rare for a figure to appear in any of his paintings. Increasingly as his understanding of the specific nature of his vision matured, he came to see that his real subject matter was not so much the scene in front of him in terms of its ingredients—trees, figures, boats, whatever—as the 'effect', that is, the particular condition of light-filled atmosphere that enfolded them all under the circumstances of the hour, making them one. Light-as-colour had to be pursued for its own sake, even if what resulted was a painting that was hardly recognisable as a picture. He was the first painter genuinely to dispense with a focal point.

To the end of his life Monet would assert that he was doing nothing but "striving to render my impressions in the face of the most fugitive effects" and he would dismiss any more elaborate accounts of his work. As his obsession deepened it became increasingly clear that subject and object, observer and observed, were locked together in a strangely intimate alliance. In one sense it didn't matter what was painted—everything from haystack to cathedral, locomotive to cloud was seen as the recipient of a particular effect of light, rendered as patches of colour laid frankly side by side. But in another sense it mattered thoroughly, for the very language with which this mysterious reduction could be brought about was itself shaped and sharpened by the themes to which he addressed himself. To paint, for example, figures out of doors and under trees (as he did many times in the late '60s and early '70s) was to look for an equivalent for the myriad units of leaves and for the arbitrary breakage of continuous forms under the impact of light and shade. Transcribing them broadly and without prejudice, the canvas itself becomes dappled with patches of colour. And this dappling does more than convey an effect: it will seem to generate an effect of itself. Or to offer another extreme example, to paint sunlight on snow meant to look for a colour equivalent for light and shadow in their purest form, totally unalloyed by local colour. The translation does more than merely describe an effect for it leads to a colour surface of a purity and intensity such that it generates first-hand responses which are in no way dependent upon what it is that is represented. But it is perhaps in his dialogue with water, to which Monet returned over and over again throughout his life, that this mysterious reciprocating transaction took place most often and most fruitfully. At Bourgival in the '60s the lively ripples in the water of *La Grenouillere* will splinter and disperse the sky, the trees, the sporting suits and summer hats, and will distribute them as colour notes throughout the lower half of the canvas. The whole scene with all its incident seems to stretch in front of us like a web in which the colour of each locality is woven into every other. Everything is everywhere; the scene is in no way to be separated out into its parts.

The story was told by Degas of seeing Monet arrive one day at his painting site on the beach at Varengeville. Monet jumps out of his carriage, takes a look at the sky and exclaims "Half an hour too late! I'll have to come back tomorrow." Everything depended upon first-hand contact with the motif and the fleeting condition of light. In his pursuit of the fugitive, he developed an astounding virtuosity in which speed and accuracy were equally matched. But from the beginning of the 1880s onwards he became increasingly distrustful of his own skill and began to look for ways of extending his command over the moment. A whole decade is marked by extreme restlessness. Continually on the move, it is as though he is hunting for more and more challenging subjects. He works on the coast in Normandy and Brittany, on the Riviera and in Italy, taking on new extremes of weather and of exotic effects of light and local colour. Around 1890 he began to develop systemmatically an idea that he had already touched upon several times, namely to paint several canvases of the same subject under varying conditions of light. The first series were of motifs found not far from the house at Giverny, the rows of poplars that stood along the banks of the Epte; and some haystacks in a field by the river. There are various accounts of his procedure. The most engaging is his own recollection: "I believed that two canvases would suffice, one for grey weather and one for sun! At that time I was painting some haystacks that had excited me and that made a magnificent group, just two steps from here. One day, I saw that my lighting had changed. I said to my stepdaughter: 'Go to the house, if you don't mind, and bring me another canvas!' She brought it to me, but a short time afterwards it was again different: 'Another!' 'Still another!' And I worked on each one only when I had my effect, that's all. It's not very difficult to understand." This account was given to the Duc de Trevise thirty years after the event. The actuality was a great deal less carefree and bland: "I am working terribly hard, struggling with a series of different effects (haystacks), but . . . the sun sets so fast that I cannot follow it . . . I am beginning to work so slowly that I am desperate, but the more I continue, the more I see that a great deal of work is necessary in order to succeed in rendering what I am seeking: 'instantaneity', especially the 'enveloppe', the same light spreading everywhere, and more than ever I am disatisfied with the easy things that come in one stroke."

It was one of these haystacks (15 were exhibited as a series in 1891) which struck the young Kandinsky with the force of a revelation when he saw it four years later at an exhibition in Moscow. Non-plussed by its vagueness—he could not at first make out what it represented—it none-the-less "engraved itself indellibly on the memory and, quite unexpectedly, hovered before the eye down to the smallest detail." Kandinsky goes on "But what was absolutely clear to me was the unexpected power . . . of the palette, which surpassed all my dreams. Painting took on a fabulous strength and splendour. And at the same time, unconsciously, the object was discredited as an indispensible element of the picture."

An even more famous series which Monet worked on a few years later would seem to confirm Kandinsky's point. These were the paintings of the facade of Rouen Cathedral. No subject imaginable could have carried denser layers of association than Rouen, the ultimate monument of Gothic architecture and the site of the coronation of the Kings of France. Yet in these paintings Monet seems, by his treatment, to be placing it on the same level as a faceless haystack, built for a season by unknown peasants. His treatment of both is given over equally to light and to a kind of dispassionate materiality in which both solid and void, light and shadow are contained within an unbroken chromatic crust.

There is something contradictory about Monet's increasing insistence upon instantaneity on one hand and his increasingly long-drawn-out, laboured procedure on the other. On the face of it there would seem to be an inevitable connection between a short-lived subject and a rapid and spontaneous style. What was it that had broken this connection and had led him to question the appropriateness of 'things that come in one stroke'? It was not, certainly, the kind of conviction that had driven Cézanne to work more and more slowly from observation. Cézanne's ambition had been to appropriate his sensations to a sense of structure derived from the art of the museums. The fleeting moment was of no interest to him: his paintings never tell us about a segment of time. With Monet the fleeting moment is everything, and yet as time went on he comes to a position where he is not capturing or responding to that fleeting moment so much as meditating upon it and trying to weave his meditations into a solid image.

If we try to imagine him working on those haystacks—some effects lasted for only twenty minutes—we have to allow for a much more contemplative attitude than that of a sharp-shooting sketcher. He is anticipating the moment; he is remembering it when it is past; above all he is looking back over what he has set down on the canvas. Inevitably memory and anticipation enter his relation to it. The moment is isolated in the stream of time, isolated, contemplated, returned to. The motif itself and the experiencing of the motif become joined.

"Monet is just an eye, but God what an eye!" For years Cézanne's *mot* was repeated as a dismissal, an apt expression of Monet's limitations, particularly in contrast to Cézanne himself. Now a century later we can begin to see more clearly the heroic quality of those limitations and of the rewards that flowed from them. At one time Monet said that he would have liked to have been born blind and to have been able to paint like a blind man who had been given his sight. He imagined the possibility of being able to experience vision with total freshness and innocence, to be able to see without knowledge, without recognition. This is perhaps how Kandinsky was able to see that Haystack canvas, at least for a few seconds. The fact is, of course, that the cases which have been studied of the blind who have gained their sight, do not reveal anything as refreshing as Monet supposed. Far from seeing the world crystal-clear and whole, those cases report a chaos of colour impressions which they have no means of organising. It takes months of work to learn to co-ordinate what is now seen with what was already understood through the other senses. Some never succeed and become depressed and long for blindness again. Seeing is a learned process which goes hand in hand with the child's learning of the world through all his senses. Furthermore, the sense of self, the ego which is uniquely separate from the outside world is sustained and defined over against a picture of the outside world which is provided by all the senses in concert.

There is no doubt that Monet knew that in embracing the sense of sight with an exclusive ardour he was, in a way, challenging and distorting common experience. He was wilfully challenging the wholeness of the senses. The enterprise verged on the monstrous. For all the sunny toughness of his vision, there is ample evidence of anxious self-questioning and feelings of incompetence and failure. Frequently in his correspondence he seems to be protesting against the unnatural course that he had set himself. In an extraordinary conversation recorded by Clemenceau (1928) Monet tells of watching by the death bed of a loved woman, when "I caught myself in the act of focussing on her temples and automatically analysing the succession of appropriately graded colours which death was imposing on her motionless face. They were blue, yellow, grey tones—tones I cannot describe. That was the point which I had reached." If, as one supposes, this experience was connected with the death of his first wife Camille, it would have taken place in 1879.

In the change that takes place in his work after about 1880 it is as though he had begun to realise that there is no way in which he could paint 'what he saw'. No painting, however strong the intention to match it to what is seen on the instant, can have more than a metaphoric relationship to what is seen on that instant. Vision is no simple process: we do not 'see' what we see, neither the retinal image nor the mental work which shapes it. Painting resembles language: it cannot replicate but it can structure.

Now Monet's painting seems to be moving towards re-creating the conditions of seeing rather than the data of what is seen. This direction can be picked up if we look at what happened to his compositions—to the way he laid the painting out and massed solids and voids within the rectangle of the canvas. Up until about 1880 his compositions are, like those of Sisley and Pissarro and his other colleagues among the landscape painters, in the continuing tradition of Corot, Boudin, Daubigny, that is to say, the result of choosing views which can be made to fit with ideas of landscape pictures carried over from an earlier studio tradition. With Pissarro, for example, the schema of classical landscape is deliberately applied out of doors. There are some canvases in which the observed data is welded into an architecture as solid and as carefully proportioned as that of a Poussin. But with Monet one feels that compositional architecture is not of great importance. He accepts the received schema loosely.

This begins to change at a certain point, as though he had resolved to reject all familiar schema and deliberately to place things unexpectedly, breaking the familiar rhythms of perspective and distance. The line of a cliff will split a picture diagonally from corner to corner; or the view point from the cliff top will be so high that the horizon of the land near-to will align exactly with the horizon of the sea, miles distant; or he will allow the form of a cliff to enter from the *top* of the picture while the foreground is occupied by glittering transparent water. By traditional criteria it is a kind of anti-composition which stresses imbalance rather than balance, flatness rather than distance, and deliberately forestalls the eye in its efforts to find a point of focus or of special intensity.

It is this feature, no doubt, which encourages later critics to describe Monet's painting as formless. We are now better able to see the point of these open, asymmetrical arrangements and to recognise their originality. What he was searching for was a structure that presented something like a screen, an allover surface, something which did not place forms at a distance but rather spread everything out in front of the eye like a tapestry unfurled. He was, of course, like most of his contemporaries, looking at Japanese prints. His is the most individual and the most pointed use of their influence: orientalism is totally transformed by this special purpose.

But as always with Monet the essential impulse comes not from art but from observation and painting from observation. Every aspect of the later paintings, the rhythm of the brush strokes no less than the way that forms are disposed or the colour is structured, evokes more and more richly the wandering, scanning movements of an eye which is looking for looking's sake. The strange, off-centre patterns that he found in Japanese art indicate a new kind of wholeness. Traditional western drawing stresses the boundaries of things, the projection of solids, the hollowing of voids and a general separation of forms from their background field. Equally, traditional western composition stresses a self-contained wholeness in the pictorial structure itself which, through its rhythmical ordering of forms and its concentration upon certain central points of focus, seems to evoke something like an ideal anatomy in the face of the viewer's own. Monet turns away from all this and in its place he embraces an overall, inclusive glance which locates each visible surface, background and foreground, figure and field, in a matrix of colour patches.

There is a vigorous interchange between the outside world and the pictorial formation. He develops a special attention for themes which seem on the face of it to be ragged, shapeless, without boundaries, such as the melting ice on the flood waters of a river, a crumbling section of cliff or a tangle of creepers and fronds which has neither centre nor edge. There are extremes of formlessness—and an equally extreme frontality which seems to be capable of radiating endlessly beyond the boundaries of the canvas. An example of the first is a painting which he made on the Creuse 1889. The picture consists of nothing but what he could see by simply looking downwards from the bank of a mountain stream. The whole canvas is filled with sparkling rushing water and above it the rocks and shapeless herbiage of the far bank. There is no exit for the eye, no outward escape. Yet the whole canvas is filled with light and air and it is as though they have been swept, along with the water, into the whipped-up surface of the canvas itself. The extreme example of the second is no less extraordinary an idea. It is one of the poplar series now in the Metropolitan Museum, New York, in which, on a nearly square canvas he places the river bank frontally about a third of the way up the canvas. The poles of four poplar trees are spaced evenly along the bank. Nothing can be seen of the crown of the trees: the poles go out of the top of the picture. The water of the river is mirror-still and the trees join with their reflections to divide the canvas regularly from top to bottom. It is like a section from a potentially endless frieze.

The cathedral facades are usually placed so that there is no way the onlooker can separate the craggy facade from the field of the canvas itself. The towers will bleed out of the top and sides, their buttresses out of the bottom, denying any purchase to the form or any way of seeing it inset within the canvas. "Not enough sky around, not enough ground" Georges Lecomte wrote when the Rouen facades were first shown. The young Signac noted: "I fully understand what these cathedrals are: marvellously executed walls." The thought could be extended to include all the subjects of his last years. Somehow he brings the outside world up close to us so that we are enfolded in its immediacy and its visual texture. Nothing is located free-standing and at a distance, or so it seems. Instead everything is close and enveloping. He overwhelms distance. We do not face the scenes he pictures so much as mingle with them, our senses streaming out into them even as they wrap us round.

The senses always operate in the present. To look at something is absolutely a different experience from remembering the look of something. Once painters began to work from direct observation, or at least, to entertain the special responses of direct observation within the content of their painting, a new time element enters painting. In as much as the work reconstructed the conditions of looking, it evokes the immediate presence of the observing eye. This is the threshold that one crosses, passing from, let us say, a Titian portrait to a Rembrandt self-portrait, whose edge, whose special particularity seems inescapably to render up a signal of Rembrandt's time—not his historical time, however, a certain year in 17th century Holland, but a more precise segment of his own breathing present.

Monet's time is inescapably there in all his paintings. In the later paintings it is no longer the time of high-speed observation and notation, but something more extended and reflective. Now there is awareness of how the perceiving eye orders and harmonises the data of the fleeting moment, an awareness which is reflected in more and more fastidious notations of colour, a more challenging pallette, in which a single and extraordinary chord of, say, cerulean, lilac and salmon pink will gather into itself all the nuances and inflexions of a single light. The motif will emerge as a structure, which is the whole canvas, dense, painted to a great depth, a totally materialised equivalent for that fleeting contact of eye and light. The passage of time is revealed as formative over against the flicker of the present.

What emerges from the great series is a deeply convincing sense of the solid, grounded, continuous nature of experience over against the discontinuous, shifting, transparent nature of the world immediately observed. Each individual canvas, with the unique observation that it contains and its special order of harmony, symbolises the ordering perception, experience stabilized. It is as though, in these late works, Monet had seen a way of including in his painting not just the data of perception but the terms upon which we build that data into our lives and make it valuable. If the earlier paintings work from the position of a mid-century materialism, the later ones seem to include in their formation something of Bergson's sense of time as duration and of his insistence on memory which "By allowing us to grasp in a single intuition multiple moments of duration . . . frees us from the movement of the flow of things, that is to say, from the rhythm of necessity."

Monet's first painting of the water garden was done in 1892, but it was not until the end of the decade that it became his principal subject. The first paintings were of the Japanese footbridge which he had built spanning the lily pond. The bridge is seen head-on, the surface of the water in raking perspective. Pampas grass, willows and larger trees fill the backgrounds. Sky rarely shows beyond the enclosing foliage. This closed-in feeling precludes a sense of the time of day or of a specific effect of light. The feeling is often drowsy and still. William C. Seitz has written of these paintings that "exotic abundance, dramatised by florid accents, is akin to the extravagant literary descriptions of Monet's friend Octave Mirbeau . . . Upon the saturated greens, blues, siennas and ochres of the pool and its wavering reflections, the lily pads and blossoms, viewed in recession, lie like a rich but tattered carpet worked with threads of pink and white."

Within a few years Monet's attention had begun to focus upon the water alone. The organising principle, firmly held to in the first paintings, and gradually relinquished, is found in the clusters and islands of blossoms and leaves which form constellations describing the surface of the water. But there are other themes present: the reflections of the surrounding trees, reflections of the sky, weeds and the golden depths of the water surrounding them. As we have seen, Monet had found himself working on equally radical compositions before, but never on this scale and never with such ambition.

For now he was beginning to feel a lessening of his physical strength. His eye-sight was beginning to give trouble; he was subject to fits of dizziness, and to bouts of depression which led him to question the worth of his efforts. He was destroying a lot of work and was obsessed with the feeling that time, his impressions were slipping away from him. Yet his hunger to capture everything was as strong as before.

Work on the water garden paintings was interrupted by trips to London between 1899 and 1901, and to Venice in 1908. New series resulted from each visit. He was now reworking more and more in the studio. His dissatisfaction increased.

On his return from Venice he prepared a group of Nympheas for exhibition. Forty-eight were shown at Durand Ruel in 1909. It was at this time that he began to speak of an ambitious plan to marshal his studies into a single scheme of decoration in a special pavilion in which the viewer would be surrounded totally by vast curving panels, representing nothing but the surface of the ponds. Claude Roger Marx wrote that he spoke of "the illusion of an endless whole, of water without horizon or bank; nerves tense from work would be relaxed there . . . and to him who lived there, that room would have offered the refuge of a peaceable meditation in the centre of a flowering aquarium."

But during the next few years the project was abandoned. His second wife died in 1911. A cataract was forming and his colour vision was becoming gradually distorted. In 1914 his son died. The war started. It was just at this point that Monet received the encouragement that he needed to re-kindle his ambition. He had spoken regretfully of the project to his old friend Georges Clemenceau who had swept aside all Monet's hesitations. A special studio was planned to take the vast canvases. This was completed two years later. A special easel was built by the side of the pond. By 1918 Monet had completed a series of about thirty panels. Clemenceau is said to have privately celebrated the armistice by visiting Giverny to select the canvases which Monet was to present to the state. By the following year he had embarked on yet another series, much larger. These were to be painted in the studio. There was also a scheme of frieze-like studies of wisteria planned.

But meanwhile his eyesight was being destroyed. Now wearing thick spectacles, he could only see in the brightest lights and he was tormented by the knowledge that he could not be sure of colour. He had to read the labels on his paint tubes. The indoor panels were being painted by a process of memory. Finally he had to stop working on them altogether for fear of ruining them. He continued to paint out of doors however, returning to the Japanese bridge, now deeply buried in wisteria, and to the tunnel-like mouth of a rose arbour. These paintings are like nothing else he had ever painted. The colour is not a balanced harmony of warm and cool colours but a smouldering tangle of reds, or, as if in compensation for the distortion that he knew was taking place, of dusky and unnatural blues. They are the only works in which his objectivity is disturbed by feeling: they are fearful images. The arch of the bridge is like the gate into a furnace and there is something almost hellish about the flickering shaggy brush-strokes of red on red. Understandably, these paintings which have been compared with the quartets of the deaf Beethoven, have a more tactile, more physical quality than anything else he did.

Finally he agreed to have one eye operated upon. The bandages were removed in February 1923. He was astonished by the way that everything became blue. By autumn he was working again. He had almost exactly three years ahead of him.

The impulse at the age of seventy to devote his remaining strength to a decorative project is not easy to understand, particularly when one considers how deeply rooted Monet's work was in realism. What motive was it that bridged the gap between a painting which purported to take all its terms from the world as it was, and a painting which set out to 'create' a self-contained world of the imagination? Above all, what of the transition from a view of painting which saw each picture as an ideal window onto a perceived world and one which saw a painting as an ideal wall enclosing a special space? The transition is doubly surprising when one reflects on the continuity of Monet's work. There are no abrupt changes in it, no redefinitions of purpose as sharp as Cézanne's espousal of Impressionism in the early seventies, to say nothing of later examples.

Clearly if we are fully to understand the significance of the last achievement we must learn to see it in the light of this continuity and not in spite of it. Of course there is a decorative element in much of impressionism. Renoir never forgot his background as a decorator of porcelain. Pissarro had periods when he applied himself to decorating fans. Monet himself had painted rococo panels in Durand Ruel's dining room in the eighties. But none of this involved a transformation of the main work.

We have seen how through the specialised vision of impressionism, Monet had freed himself, in a sense, from normal ties. He could look at anything. His 'discovery' of the universality of light and of the fact that in painting, light could be translated directly into colour, gave him a kind of omnipotence. He was like an alchemist. And the very fact that the source of his power was his dispassionate, observing eye—the organ which spans distance, which 'takes in' whatever it lights upon, which carries the instant in its glance—gave a freedom and a modernity to his position which no earlier painter, however Protean had ever enjoyed. In the best of Monet's painting there is a sense of access to the world—not only that he is on good terms with the particular portion that he is painting, but that he sees that portion as a section of something much larger. His vision is commanding and yet, unlike any of his predecessors, he does not stamp it with his own poetic image. His command operates through the terms of painting itself, and the perceptual functions that it transcribes and symbolises. This is his modernity, the utterly radical element.

When we reflect on the vast range of his activity—the places he painted, out of doors, in all weathers, from pavements, windows, riverbanks, punts, Honfleur to Venice, Antibes to Norway, Hyde Park to the Gare St Lazare, his lights, seasons, bricks, rocks, flowers, girders, clouds, smokes, waves, meadows, mountains, rivers, canals, trees, bridges, etc.—it seems that there is something imperial about his consuming appetite and energy. All this was within power, the power of his eye. All this paid its contribution to his power—he commanded it and fed off it. When finally, with his own property, he was able really to create a garden, deflect a river, plant trees, it seems but an extension of his extraordinary power—an extension of which the corollary was not just to paint further views but to create a 'place' through the total command of his painting.

As always, nature shapes sensation, which in turn shapes the painting, which in turn shapes sensation, an endless dialogue. The *Nymphéas* seem to be in close-up; we seem so far as there is a view-point, to be looking downward, deep into the spread of water. There is no horizon, no perspective, only an occasional sense of surface. Water seems to embrace us: a single canvas from the last *Nymphéas* is as enveloping as the entire scheme. The eye drifts, curves, falling slowly then recovering, as an accent catches it. Nothing seems designed or strained after in these vast surfaces, for all the pain and effort that was expended on them. Nothing is constructed. It is rather as if in working one's way across and between the shifting surface, the eye discovers a location for everything by its own efforts. A concentration of bluey-violet seems to float slowly downwards; perhaps it is a pale cloud inverted in the pond. One has hardly isolated it from the texture of the whole before it has given way to a golden thicket—reflected trees, or a tangle of weeds struck by the warm underwater light. The lilies are themselves like clouds, opalescent, broken, fragments of sky and watery depth woven into their thick crumbling texture.

Monet : Living and Painting in Giverny

Claire Joyes

"Monsieur Monet que l'hiver ni
L'été sa vision ne leurre
Habite en peignant Giverny
Sis auprès de Vernon, dans l'Eure."

Address written on an envelope actually delivered to Monet in Giverny.

The Giverny story had its beginnings in the summer of 1876, when Claude Monet paid his first visit to the Château de Rottenbourg, Ernest Hoschedé's country house at Montgeron.

Ernest Hoschedé was a wealthy business man, a director of several companies including Au Gagne-Petit, a fashionable Paris department store. He was, moreover, an enlightened and generous patron of the arts, who appreciated Impressionist painting while it was still considered alarmingly avant-garde and made friends with many of the artists of that movement. At a time when everyone was trying to forget the Franco-Prussian War and its aftermath, the Hoschedés' considerable wealth, squads of discreet and efficient servants and longstanding convictions enabled them to live a life which was a strange mixture of ostentatious fêtes, charitable works, patronage of the avant-garde, worldly eccentricities and religious fervour.

At Montgeron Hoschedé and his wife, Alice, entertained in great style, giving parties to which guests came from Paris by special train. In the quieter intervals they welcomed chosen friends, invited for their personal gifts and qualities rather than social status. Regular visitors to Rottenbourg included the publisher Georges Charpentier and his wife, the Carolus-Durans (country neighbours of the Hoschedés), Edouard Manet and his wife, Louis Baudry and Jean-Jacques Henner. Even Alfred Sisley sometimes put in an appearance at Montgeron. At Rottenbourg one met both landscape painters, enthusiasts for working out of doors, and portrait painters who felt more at home in the drawing-room where they would take it in turns to sit for one another's portraits.

Claude Monet was a very special guest. Hoschedé had already bought some of his paintings, but the two men knew each other only slightly. Monet was then a controversial but not unknown painter. His works had been accepted only twice at the Salon, but two of his pictures had received much attention, especially from Emile Zola: *Road in Fontainebleau Forest* in 1865 and *Camille*, a portrait of his future wife Camille Doncieux, in 1866. The Salon of 1867 rejected his *Women in the Garden* and after 1869 there seemed little chance that his newer works would be accepted. At that time there was no hope for any artist outside the Salon, but despite this, Monet, weary of being at the mercy of official selection committees, had decided not to submit any more paintings. It therefore became urgently necessary to find some alternative way to show his work and in 1874 he organised an exhibition in the Paris studio of the photographer Nadar. Among the 30 other participants were Boudin, Cézanne, Degas, Morisot, Pissarro, Renoir and Sisley. The title of one of Monet's paintings shown in this exhibition, *Impression, Sunrise* (1872) was held up to ridicule, especially by Louis Leroy, critic of the journal *Le charivari*. The whole group of painters was inevitably dubbed the 'Impressionists', an insult which gave a name to the movement. The public also greeted the exhibition with derision and saw it only as the provocative gesture of a set of eccentrics.

At Rottenbourg Monet rose early in the mornings and after lunch seemed in no hurry to return to his outdoor subjects on which he worked assiduously. He preferred to wait until the late afternoon when the light was less intense. Meanwhile he would rest or linger in the company of his hosts. It was during this period that Hoschedé bought some of his new paintings, among them, *The White Turkeys* and *The Pond at Montgeron*. The Hoschedés and Monet got on remarkably well. None of them were aware how much their relationship, a few weeks old, was to mean in their lives. Back in Paris, in the autumn of 1876, they continued to see each other and the acquaintance developed into a closer friendship. Monet received his friends in his studio and the Hoschedés continued to entertain on a lavish scale, with the same carefree generosity. That year they gave a memorable masked dinner at which Madame Charpentier wore a fine mask, painted for her by Renoir, while Renoir himself and Monet, an irrepressible pair when together, made hideous disguises for themselves.

Hoschedé's ruin

The Hoschedés enjoyed a good life and it seemed an idyllic existence. In fact, all was not well with Hoschedé's business affairs. He had concealed the gravity of the situation from his wife and their life style remained unaltered. But for the second time in two years he had been threatened with a relegation to a minority shareholding by his fellow directors at Au Gagne-Petit.

Early in the summer of 1877 he was summoned to appear before his business associates. Unable to justify his position he left home without telling his family or associates. A chance meeting with a friend deterred him from attempting suicide; he took refuge in Belgium, writing thence to his wife in the utmost confusion and despair. "My beloved wife!" he wrote, "what can I call you, what may I call you now? . . . I struggled like a giant for a whole month . . . I lost my head . . . I wanted to kill myself . . . I can't stay in Paris. Am I to go on living for your sake and that of our beloved children? . . . Don't curse me . . . Tell me to take heart or tell me to disappear . . . Let no one try to find me, or I shall kill myself . . ."

Alice's comfortable universe collapsed; she had been deserted with five children and another on the way. The creditors and partners of Au Gagne-Petit were entitled to the Hoschedés' remaining assets. The Château de Rottenbourg, Alice's own property, was sold, the furniture seized and their collection of paintings by Monet, Manet, Renoir and Sisley auctioned by court order. Twelve important works by Monet were sold, including *Saint-Germain l'Auxerrois*, for absurdly small prices. All the servants were dismissed, but one devoted housemaid insisted on staying with Alice.

Alice's final appeal was to one of her sisters in Biarritz, and with her housemaid and five children she set out by train for the coast. Halfway there the train was halted while her sixth child, Jean-Pierre, was born. The family at Biarritz agreed to make her a small allowance, largely for the children's education. Back in Paris she experienced poverty for the first time; to earn a little money she took in dressmaking for her friends.

The Monets and the Hoschedés

For the Monets meanwhile nothing had altered. Their financial difficulties were, as always, acute. His art was still misunderstood, and there was no help to be had either from his own relatives or those of his wife.

In 1878, despite the loss of Rottenbourg, the Hoschedé and Monet families decided to spend the summer together in the country and rented a house at Vétheuil where, instead of staying a few months, they stayed three years. It was far cheaper living in the country and Monet kept on discovering new subjects. As always happened when a landscape inspired him he worked at it to the point of exhaustion.

It was at Vétheuil, in winter, for instance, that a brief thaw, lasting only a few hours, enabled him to produce the series of paintings of *The Break-Up of the Ice*.

There were, however, periods not of mere impoverishment but real destitution, when Monet would barter a canvas for a pair of boots and leave his paintings as a pledge with the tradesmen. There was only one smart dress in the Vétheuil wardrobe, so Alice and Camille would take turns to go to Paris. Dignity was maintained, whatever the circumstances. During this period Camille gave birth to a second son who was named Michel. Shortly after she fell gravely ill and in 1879 she died from tuberculosis. For a time the dazed and distressed Monet left the care of his children to Alice Hoschedé.

Although genteel by birth and upbringing, with sensitive and somewhat mystical tendencies, Alice Hoschedé had shown a strength and unusual dignity in coping with desertion and financial ruin. Now she revealed even more inner resources as she faced a new kind of situation. With immense practical wisdom she took on not merely the rebuilding of a family life from two shattered homes and the education of eight children, but also the encouragement and sustenance of Monet himself, in whose artistic genius she believed.

Vétheuil, however, offered no educational facilities; and for the sake of the children's schooling they all moved to Poissy. Monet found it difficult to work there. The landscape, and presumably the light, did not suit him. He detested each of the houses in which they successively lived, and when summer came, in order to escape from "that horrible Poissy", they went to Pourville, by the sea, where he hoped to be able to paint more and to "do some good work" at last.

The lease in Poissy expired in April much to Monet's delight, even though he had no idea where they would go next. His one idea was to get away. His wish was to stop moving house, to find a village he liked well enough to make him want to stop and paint, at some distance from Paris without being too remote. Irresistibly attracted by the Seine valley, Monet searched despondently for another village. He had pleasant memories of small villages in the Vernon district which he had once discovered during long rambles and boat-trips down the Seine from Vétheuil.

The train that took him from Poissy to Vernon in April 1883 followed the windings of the Seine. Depressed and worried, Monet recalled his recent misfortunes: the summer at Pourville when his hopes of painting out of doors had been constantly frustrated by the horrible weather and the flooding of the Seine at Poissy which had added a further complication to his life. ". . . I'm no longer a painter," he had written to Durand-Ruel, "but a life-boatman, a ferryman, a removal man . . . We're literally under water . . ." It maddened him, for, as he went on: "I can't think of painting and yet there are things which would be most interesting to do." The servants had left in a panic, and Monet helped Mme Hoschedé in the house; they had to open the ground floor doors to let the water circulate freely, and then take refuge on the first floor; the house was only accessible by boat. All this was a waste of precious painting time, and Monet's aggravation was increased by his recent one-man show at Durand-Ruel's on February 15th, which had been, as he himself admitted, a total flop—"un four complet".

After a number of journeys on the little train that ran through the Epte valley, Monet's systematic exploration of villages succeeded when he was on the point of losing heart. He came back to Poissy one day in high spirits. He had found a house at last, at Giverny. All that was needed now was energy to organise the move.

The business took nearly ten days. Besides endless comings and goings between Poissy and Giverny, loaded with luggage, Monet had also to see to the transport of his boats. Finally he left for Giverny on April 29th with some of the children. He had to leave the others at Poissy with Mme Hoschedé, for at the last moment, short of money, they had been unable to take the train, until Durand-Ruel came to the rescue.

Giverny

The train journey from Vernon to Giverny reveals the Seine, fairly wide in this area, with hills that rise on either side; densely cultivated on the south side which gets the sun and steeper and more wooded on the other.

In the valley run two streams: the Ru and the Epte, the latter a narrow stream that serves as division between two provinces, Normandy and the Ile-de-France. Here and there a line of willows and poplars betray the winding course of some tiny tributary. There is nothing flat nor bare about the country; everything is rather wild, dense and abundant.

Between the water and the hills, instead of huddling dutifully round the church, Giverny sprawls lengthwise, its low houses, roofed with small brown mossy tiles, surrounded by gardens, apple orchards and cultivated fields. In the very heart of the village thickset hedges jealously guard individual plots. As in all great river valleys, the light is soft and quick to change, sharpening outlines or blurring shapes, ceaselessly altering the look of things.

A few hundred metres from Giverny station, in the part of the village known as the 'Pressoir', the cider press, stood Monet's house, between the ruelle Leroy and the rue de l'Amiscourt. It was a homely, unpretentious dwelling — a long, tallish building with a low barn at either end, covered in pink rough-cast, with grey shutters.

The house had formerly belonged to a rich tradesman from Guadeloupe and there was something faintly exotic about the pink rough-cast under the rainy Normandy sky. The garden was somewhat prim, with absurd clipped box bushes. Two rather long, stiff flower beds ran parallel to a broad central walk, edged with spruce and cypresses that gave an unexpectedly solemn look to the place, and sloped down to the lower road, the chemin du Roy. Beyond lay meadows of lush grass, perenially green, water-logged, thick with flowers in the spring and surrounded by willows and poplars. Only the linden trees and a couple of splendid yews at the head of the main walk found favour in Monet's and Alice's eyes. On the whole, it was a typical provincial bourgeois garden, unimaginatively laid out and quite devoid of botanical interest.

The arrival at Giverny coincided with news of Manet's death (April 30th, 1883). It brought shock and grief to the household, and Monet left immediately for Paris to be one of the pall-bearers at the funeral. Nevertheless life at Giverny had to take shape and a daily routine was established. As the weather was fine, meals could be taken out of doors, with cane chairs and a big table set out under the linden trees. Summer was near and Monet set about organising the kitchen garden, and creating a more attractive flower garden. There was no time to be lost if vegetables were to grow that year, as well as flowers that he could paint when the weather kept him indoors.

Monet had firm ideas about the flower garden. He hated anything that looked formal and it was decided that the clipped box bushes must go. But there were tremendous arguments amongst the household about the spruces and cypresses. A visit from Caillebotte, a fellow painter and one of Monet's closest friends, was expected and they decided to ask his

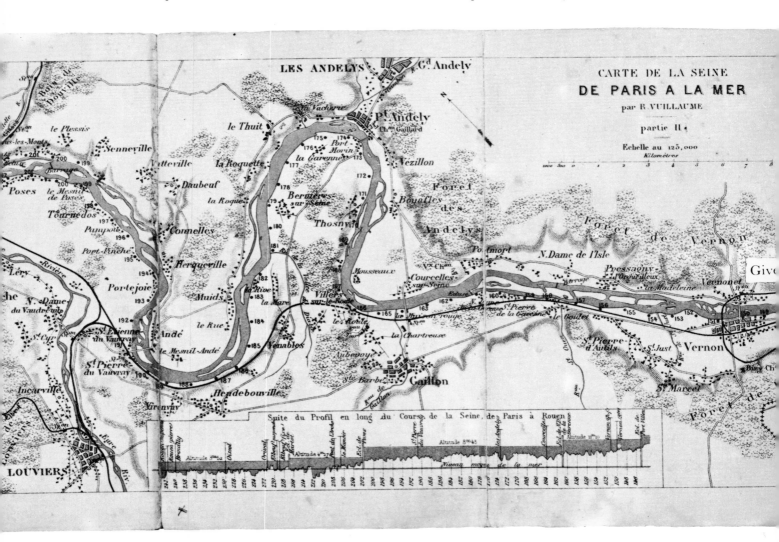

opinion. It was he who had given Monet his love of gardening. They had been neighbours at Argenteuil in the mid-1870's and Caillebotte had delighted Monet with his passion for painting, boats and botany—in fact, he owned a magnificent hothouse.

It was planned that Caillebotte should sail his yacht the *Casse-Museau* from Argenteuil to Giverny where Monet would join him on board. They were to spend a few days together painting and then sail down the Seine to call on their friend, the writer Octave Mirbeau, who shared their passion for gardening. Mirbeau had written Monet a characteristically whimsical letter: ". . . I'm glad you're bringing Caillebotte, we'll talk about gardens. Art and literature are all nonsense. Earth is the only thing that matters . . . I can spend hours staring at a clod of earth . . . I love humus like a woman . . ."

Impatient to resume his work, Monet wanted to find a suitable place to moor his boats. Apart from bare necessities the household had little furniture, but they had no less than four craft: one big boat with a cabin, which served as a studio; the *Norvégienne*, a round-stemmed rowing-boat; and two mahogany skiffs.

At the mouth of the Epte where it reaches the Seine there are a number of tiny islands with shores of fine sand. One such is the Ile aux Orties—Nettle Island, which Monet discovered on his first long expedition from Giverny on foot. He was delighted with this remote but lush island and here, with the help of the boys, he decided to moor the boats.

The family and the village

Giverny offered the family many delights. The children explored the village whose narrow lanes bore medieval names: the Pressoir, the Chenevières, the rue aux Juifs, the rue des Chandeliers, the rue Messire Jean Coulbeaux, the chemin de la Dîme, as well as the rue de l'Amsicourt and the chemin du Roy.

They picnicked and went for long walks in the rich meadows and up the hillside paths, reaching plateaux from which they could look down on the wide expanse of water. The

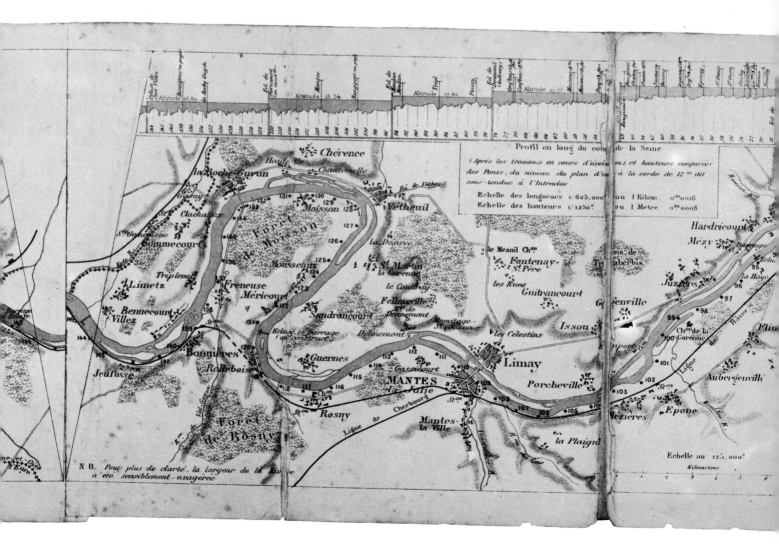

walk to Nettle Island remained their favourite expedition, though it was a long trek, single file, through cultivated fields to reach the Seine. On several occasions they found the *Norvégienne* adrift, and they had to retrieve it several kilometres downstream at the lock. Monet's current task was to build a shelter to house the boats and his painting equipment. With the boy's help he constructed a floating landing-stage to which the studio boat could be securely moored. On family expeditions to the islands the children, once there, would scatter off to play or wander on their own, set their fishing lines or clean out the boats.

Most of the inhabitants of Giverny were peasants; although not openly hostile, they were prepared to make the newcomers pay a good price for their favours. As in every village, there were some remarkable figures: the traditional idiot, the inveterate poacher, a bogus beggar-woman, and a half crazy witch who lived in a cave in the nearby hamlet of Falaise.

The Givernois were somewhat bemused by the Monet family; eccentric and bohemian in appearance, they were neither country folk nor town gentry with the girls in their bright check cotton dresses with an endless succession of parasols, the boys wearing pale pink felt hats. The only obviously respectable member of the family was Mme Hoschedé, an impressive figure in her dresses of sober printed foulard.

The peasants clearly did not consider painting a proper occupation and even though Monet liked to wear sabots and a beret, he was not popular. Reserved by nature and sparing of speech, the villagers considered him proud and aloof. There was considerable ill feeling.

The villagers claimed compensation for the supposed damage done to their crops by the family, as they trailed through privately owned fields on their way to Nettle Island. Monet was forced to pay, on pain of being cut off from his favourite retreat. Later, when he was painting haystacks the peasants threatened to demolish them, and when he undertook his series of poplars they took pleasure in telling him that the trees were to be cut down. By paying a sum of money he was able to persuade them not to carry out their threat. Monet began to react to this insidious malevolence with contempt and learned to ignore his neighbours.

A day in a painter's life

Monet was always up by four or five in the morning; he would open the window, the curtains were never drawn, and study the sky. Whatever the temperature he would always take a cold bath. He used to say that he loved getting up, that he often felt like returning to his bed for the pleasure of leaving it again. There were often other reasons for going back to bed; when he was disappointed by his previous day's work, or when the weather looked threatening, he would retreat under his blankets in anger and stay in his room all day, refusing to come down to meals and rejecting all Alice's attempts to console him. This situation might go on for days. Monet was often a difficult character, irascible and moody, always dissatisfied with his work, liable to fly into a temper over a broken flower, an unexpected visitor, some inexpertise in the kitchen, and above all by the variations in weather and light. When Monet was in such tempers nobody dared speak a word or make a noise; the tension was only broken when he reappeared radiant and full of fresh zeal for painting.

The landscape at Giverny fascinated him. He spent a long while exploring, walking over hills and through valleys, in marshes and meadows, among streams and poplars. Or, drifting down the quiet river in his boat he would watch with a hunter's concentration for the precise moment when light shimmered on grass or on silver willow leaves or on the surface of the water. Suddenly or by degrees his motif would be revealed to him.

Monet's main stimulus was the close study of nature—of streams and quivering hedges, hills and green meadows, the impalpable lilac haze that hangs above the Seine at dawn, figures dissolving in a diaphanous atmosphere, the glow of sunset over the marshes or the frozen stillness of a Normandy winter. When Monet began working in earnest at Giverny, the whole household revolved round his timetable and was organised to fit in with the rhythm of his work. The first improvements to the house had been to the studio: a huge window now flooded it with light, an interior staircase and a new door were put in, and the floor of beaten earth had been replaced by pitchpine floorboards.

Monet prepared for his hard day's work with a substantial breakfast: the best tea from the Compagnie Coloniale or Kardomah's, a taste acquired when he was in England in 1870; milk, cheese, cold meat—a Dutch habit; eggs, grilled sausage, toast and marmalade. Breakfast was an important ceremony and could be a delightful one, if Monet was in a good mood. He would invite one of the children to share it, and to go along with him to help carry his equipment. Blanche, who loved painting, was his most assiduous assistant. She often accompanied him at work, and Monet and his companion would load their gear on to a wheelbarrow and make their way through the dewy countryside to their hut on Nettle Island, to watch the sun rise; or else would get themselves driven in a horse drawn cart to some more remote spot. Monet, who hated the very idea of painting lessons, would give her advice. They seldom chose the same subject, but their easels were never very far apart.

The household conformed to a timetable as strict as that of a monastery. Monet came home at eleven sharp for lunch, which was served at noon after the bell had been rung twice. He could not stand unpunctuality, and would start coughing nervously if kept waiting. After the meal he would allow himself a brief respite, drinking a cup of coffee and a glass of home-made plum brandy. If the light had not changed too drastically he would go back to paint out of doors, otherwise he stayed in the studio. The dinner bell interrupted him again at seven o'clock, and he invariably went to bed at 9.30 so as to be at work very early next day. During the holidays the rhythm was more relaxed; the whole family joined Monet on his painting expeditions. At Nettle Island he worked and sometimes played with the children, while Alice sat calmly sewing. There were picnics, boating, tennis and swimming.

Monet's financial difficulties

The sole support of the Monet family had for years been the picture dealer Paul Durand-Ruel—'Monsieur Durand' whom Monet first met in London in 1870. By supporting the Impressionists Durand-Ruel had ventured his whole fortune, jeopardised his reputation as a talent scout and come close to ruin.

Monet, like many of his fellow painters, often received advances on pictures that were not even begun. These provided the money to pay Jean's school fees and some living expenses. Troisgros, the dealer in artists' materials, sent his bills to Durand-Ruel's office in the rue Lafitte, as did Monet's tailor. Money orders from Durand-Ruel, together with Mme Hoschedé's personal income and the occasional sale to some private collector, enabled Monet to go on working without real anxiety, but were inadequate to defray the expenses of their somewhat refined way of living.

The whole family was accustomed to living free from practical concerns. Monet, often working for months on a single work, seemed unable actually to 'finish' a painting. Just as he was about to fasten down the crates for despatch to Durand-Ruel, he would be siezed with doubt, discover some inadequacy, and withdraw the unsatisfactory work. His friends deplored this lifelong habit: Mirbeau warned him against his crazy perfectionism and Geffroy, the critic and later biographer of Monet begged him to stop scraping away at his landscapes and figures. By dint of deliberate or impulsive retouching, Monet often ruined his work. Most of the time he would heed no one's advice, but would treat his paintings with the utmost brutality, scraping and lacerating them in a fury, and would finally pile them in a corner of the garden and set fire to them. Such autos-da-fé horrified the family, but this masochistic gesture purged Monet, and he would then resume work.

In 1884 Durand-Ruel was forced to withhold support for a while, his own banker having gone bankrupt. Depression overwhelmed Monet; of course he would go on to the end burning and tearing up his canvases, but in the meantime he would have to produce work which he lacked time to judge. On the other hand he would never consent to give his work a more finished appearance in order to please the public and sell his pictures. In 1884 he wrote to Durand-Ruel: ". . . I really believe we're faced with destitution again in spite of your admirable perseverence . . . one cannot live without money". Even when the hateful and humiliating quest for buyers had begun again, he could not bear to economise; he had to have a kitchen garden well stocked with the choicest vegetables, a couple of maids in the kitchen, the best of food and wine, while Parisian tailors went on making Alice's dresses and cloaks, and Monet's suits, of high quality materials, and in the summer the whole family would go off for a holiday to Forges-les-Eaux or Salies-de-Béarn.

Durand-Ruel went to America in March 1886 to organise an exhibition of French Impressionist painting in New York, which opened on April 10th and showed 310 works, including 50 by Monet. The reaction was encouraging. The American public, though puzzled, sought to understand these new works. Monet however, without money during Durand-Ruel's absence, sold some of his work in the meantime to Georges Petit's rival gallery in Paris.

A second Impressionist exhibition opened in New York in May, 1887. This was a 'succès d'estime' and in the same year Durand-Ruel opened his New York branch on Fifth Avenue. Monet disapproved of Durand's American venture, for he felt very strongly about his works leaving France permanently. A certain coolness had impaired Monet's friendship with Durand-Ruel, initially because of Monet's dealings with Georges Petit. Monet had exhibited with Petit in the 3rd and 4th Expositions Internationales in 1884 and 1885 and had been reproached by Durand-Ruel for arranging a one-man show with Petit. In 1888 Monet exhibited ten landscapes of Antibes at another gallery, Boussod and Valadon, in an exhibition organised by Vincent van Gogh's brother, Théo. The rift between Monet and Durand-Ruel widened.

Semi-official recognition came to Monet in 1889 with the joint exhibition with Rodin held at Georges Petit's fashionable gallery on the rue de Sèze. There were 66 paintings with a preface to the catalogue by Octave Mirbeau. Monet was enraged because Durand-Ruel refused to lend works from his collection, but the exhibition was nonetheless an enormous popular success. Three months later Théo van Gogh obtained the record price of 9,000 francs for a Monet.

In 1890 Monet was back with Durand-Ruel, but on a more business-like and less friendly basis. In the spring and summer of that year he continued work on his two important series of *Poplars* and *Haystacks* and in May, 1891 showed 22 paintings, including 15 *Haystacks*, at Durand-Ruel's. All were sold within three days for prices between 3,000 and 4,000 francs. Monet, now fifty-one, was commanding the highest prices of any of the Impressionists. From this time on he developed a tougher business sense, and though most of his output went to Durand, he avoided a formal agreement and continued to sell to other dealers as it suited him.

Monet was already painting the series of the Cathedral in Rouen when reports of the success of his exhibition of *Poplars* at Durand-Ruel's gallery reached him. He received letters asking for the first of his Rouen paintings, which nobody had yet seen. Monet, who spent years working on each of his series, must have smiled inwardly at this reaction. Pissarro wrote: "What a lovely thing, those three arrangements of poplars in the evening light, how painterly and how decorative!"

A quiet life

Monet's life in Giverny was dominated by the demands of his painting and any spare time was taken up with gardening. One of his lasting passions was for water, an eradicable fascination going back to his boyhood in Le Havre. This had surely determined his choice of riverside homes at Argenteuil, Vétheuil and Poissy and even Giverny, overlooking as it did a sleepy branch of the Epte. Indeed it is surprising that he never chose to live in some recess of the Normandy coast to which he constantly returned, with fresh admiration, to paint. So obsessed was he by love of the sea that he said: ". . . I should like to be always in front of it or on it, and when I die, to be buried in a buoy."

Boating was part of the family's way of life. They took part in the September boat races, for which they practised for months before. When the great day came the boats, loaded with extraordinary apparatus and lavish picnic baskets, would set off amid tumultuous shouts of encouragement.

In 1893 Monet, Mirbeau and Blanche were passengers for a whole week on the liner *Normandie* on its trip to Cherbourg to witness a visit from the Tsar, Alexander III, escorted by part of the Russian fleet. At sea a ferocious storm blew up. While the bravest souls deserted the deck Monet and Blanche clad in oilskins remained, huddled in securely fastened deck chairs, watching the wild fury of the waves with excitement. Recalling the trip years later it was the memory of the storm that remained and not the pageantry and display of the Tsar's visit.

Monet seldom went to Paris. He hated and despised the petty scheming and intrigues of social life. Sometimes, however, he took Alice to wrestling matches, of which she was particularly fond; also they often went to concerts and were close friends of Emmanuel Chabrier. They were at the first nights of all Mirbeau's plays, and of Rostand's *Chantecler*, in which their friend Lucien Guitry played the lead; they heard Chaliapin sing *Boris Godunov* at the Opéra and saw Pavlova dance *The Dying Swan* and Loie Fuller perform her sensational 'serpentine dance'. They dined at Prunier's or Marguery's and sometimes managed to extract from the chef a fabulous recipe such as the delectable *sole Marguery*. It was all a far cry from the time when Monet, living in Paris, had frequented such squalid eating houses as Monsieur Fromage's where the main dish was concocted from cheese leftovers, or another restaurant in the rue de Rennes where the cutlery was chained to the table to protect it from the impoverished clientele.

Back at Giverny Monet would exchange his city clothes for his country garments. When he went painting he liked to wear a beret and sabots. His suits were usually made of sober English flecked material, of unfashionable but highly individual cut. His choice of pastel coloured cambric shirts, finely pleated, the cuffs projecting over his slender hands, with a pleated jabot instead of a tie betrayed the touch of the dandy. His trousers were fastened at the ankle with three buttons, and his boots of fine quality leather, though by no means military looking, were always made to measure by the bootmaker who supplied the cavalry regiment of Vernon. Monet seldom felt the cold or wore a knitted garment, except on cool autumn evenings when he would throw a jersey over his shoulders. He was conservative about his dress and so neat and careful that there was never a trace of paint on his clothes, any more than on his studio floor which always gleamed brightly.

Monet was a domestic tyrant, pernickety about the time for picking young beans, flying into a temper if some premature blossom had altered the subject of a painting; but at the same time his generosity and simplicity were as well known as his easily aroused temper. He was a loyal friend, reserved and yet warm-hearted, discreet and considerate, tender towards the unfortunate and indignant at injustice. Equally prone to absolute passivity and to extreme violence, he was driven to fury and roused to action by two events.

The first concerned Manet's painting *Olympia*. Manet is said to have regarded this as his greatest work and many of his friends agreed. In 1889 there were rumours of its sale to an American collector. Monet, alarmed that the painting might leave the country, decided to organise a private subscription to purchase the painting for the Louvre, where he and John Sargent believed it rightfully belonged. Throughout the year Monet tirelessly besieged his friends and acquaintances to contribute to the fund. The response was largely favourable; but there were surprising reactions from two of Manet's closest supporters. Emile Zola, who as far back as 1867, had praised Manet's talent, would not respond to the appeal. Antonin Proust, in an article in the *Figaro*, made it clear that he did not support the move either. Moreover, he suggested that Monet and his friends were not motivated by interest in the work itself, but in an oblique way were trying to help Manet's widow, who was in financial straits. Monet was pained and angered by this "shocking and spiteful" article; for Proust had not only been a Minister of Fine Arts but had also been a pall-bearer at Manet's funeral. "He thinks it's natural," Monet wrote to Geffroy, "that Manet should not occupy the place he merits, whereas twenty fifth-rate daubers have all the glory." Nor did Monet mince words with Proust; offended by them, Proust challenged the painter to a duel which fortunately did not take place. Monet's seconds, Duret and Geffroy, prudently arranged a meeting between the two adversaries. Proust changed his mind, subscribed towards the purchase of the picture and promised apologies to Mme Manet. Finally, about 20,000 francs were raised by the subscribers, including Degas, Duret, Lautrec, Mallarmé, Puvis de Chavannes, Renoir, Rodin and Durand-Ruel. The painting was placed in the Luxembourg Palace in 1890, but it was not until 1907 that Clemenceau, was able to arrange for it to be transferred to the Louvre.

The second event to incur Monet's anger was the Dreyfus affair which contaminated French politics from 1894 for many years to follow. The whole country was at odds; it shattered families, friendships and old associations and even the Giverny household could not avoid becoming involved. In December 1894 a young Jewish officer, Captain Alfred Dreyfus, was tried and convicted of treason for selling military secrets to the Germans. His family and many others were convinced of his innocence, but he was convicted on very slender evidence. When, in 1896, new evidence pointing to the guilt of another officer, Esterhazy, came to light, the Dreyfus supporters, including Monet's friends Clemenceau and Emile Zola, launched a massive campaign demanding a retrial. Monet, a convinced Dreyfusard, joined them. The accusations against Esterhazy resulted in a court martial that acquitted him of treason in January 1898. In protest against the verdict, Zola published, on the 13th January 1898, his famous letter *J'accuse* in Clemenceau's newspaper *L'Aurore*. In it he attacked the army for illegally covering up its mistaken conviction of Dreyfus—an action for which he was tried and found guilty of libel. Zola, on the advice of friends, fled to England.

Relations between Monet and Zola had not always been cordial. Although in the '60's and '70's when Monet was in desperate financial straits Zola, by no means rich himself, had helped Monet on several occasions, the publication of Zola's novel, *L'œuvre*, in 1886 caused an apparently irreconcilable break. The hero of Zola's novel was an Impressionist painter whose dreams and ambitions end in failure and suicide because of his lack of creative talent. Zola's own notes reveal that the portrait was based partly on Manet and partly on Cézanne, the two painters whom he knew intimately. Most readers identified the hero with Manet, for Cézanne was at that time relatively unknown. But Cézanne saw in the novel a disturbing echo of his own life. He felt not only betrayed but also acutely aware of Zola's pity for him because he had not achieved success. Zola had misunderstood the aims of the Impressionists and worse, he had been disloyal. Cézanne wrote to thank Zola for the copy of *L'œuvre*. It was a farewell letter, which ended a thirty year friendship. The two were never to meet again.

Monet was brutally frank in his reactions:

> "You were kind enough to send me a copy of *L'œuvre*. I am much obliged to you. I have always had great pleasure in reading your books, and this one interested me doubly because it raises questions of art for which we have been fighting for such a long time. I have read it, and I remain troubled, disturbed, I must admit. You took care, intentionally, that not one of your characters should resemble any of us, but in spite of that, I am afraid that the press and the public, our enemies, may use the name of Manet, or at least our names to prove us to be failures . . . . I have read *L'œuvre* with very great pleasure . . . . but I have been struggling fairly long and I am afraid that in the moment of succeeding, our enemies may make use of your book to deal us a knockout blow."

Despite this Monet believed Zola's publication of *J'accuse* was a brilliant and courageous manifesto, an opinion which was shared by Pissarro. Of his other painter friends Degas joined the militarists, turned anti-Semitic and thenceforth avoided them, while Cézanne failed to rally behind Zola.

The invasion of Giverny

The Giverny household was no longer troubled with financial problems after the mid-1880's. In 1890 their landlord, Singeot, put the house up for sale and Monet bought it without a moment's hesitation. Old Singeot, a great drinker of the local wine, known as *cailloutin*, was a man of few but firmly held ideas who knew that his tenant was very fond of the house and sold it to him for the tidy sum of 22,000 francs. Monet guaranteed to pay in three years. After 1890 money from the sale of pictures was spent on improvements to the house, on building a second studio beside the linden trees, and on beautifying the garden with tropical plants, flowering trees and hothouses.

Monet worked with little respite, cutting himself off from the family except at mealtimes. They could tell at once from the way he walked, or from the first words he uttered, whether his work had gone well. At meals they would discuss the trivial events of daily life, the news from Jean in Switzerland, from Jacques in Norway and from Germaine at her convent boarding school. Monet encouraged Jean-Pierre and Michel in their flower collection, which was, by now, of some scientific interest. On holidays he would organise trips for them to unfamiliar places where they could look for fresh specimens. The boys had, in fact, undertaken some curious cross-breeding experiments in the garden, with results that were sometimes splendid and sometimes disastrous. One day there appeared a very handsome poppy, a cross between an oriental specimen and a common field poppy. It spread abundantly in the flower beds. The boys, who were compiling a *Flora of Vernon and La Roche-Guyon*, consulted their adviser, the Abbé Anatole Toussaint, the local parish priest and a botanist of note, who decided that this cross-fertilisation, though accidental, should bear the name *Papaver Moneti*.

In his early days at Giverny, Monet's contact with his fellow painters was maintained at the monthly dinners held in Paris at the Café Riche. The fare was excellent, and the company included art critics and writers—Mallarmé and Huysmans were often present—as well as Renoir, Sisley, Caillebotte and Pissarro. The often stormy discussions included art, literature, politics and philosophy and arguments begun here were sometimes continued by letter. Monet was particularly interested in literature and would discuss Victor Hugo and Flaubert. He read Maeterlinck, recommended to him at one such dinner by Mirbeau and Mallarmé, and was a passionate admirer of Balzac, Ibsen, Tolstoy and Edmond de Goncourt.

Back at Giverny he looked forward to visits from close friends, which he found both relaxing and stimulating. They, moreover, tolerated his moods, finding him on some occasions full of enthusiasm and proudly displaying his garden; on others, sulky and depressed about either his painting or the weather which prevented him from working.

Although Monet was an avowed atheist, his only close friend from the village was the Abbé Toussaint, who not only supervised the boys' botanical researches, but was someone with whom Monet could discuss botany. All his other friends were old acquaintances from Le Havre, Paris and London. Pissarro came over from nearby Eragny-sur-Epte and Renoir when he was staying at La Roche-Guyon in 1885 and 1886 often came to Giverny. The Sisleys and their children and John Singer Sargent were regular visitors, as was Monet's great comrade, Caillebotte. Later, after meeting Geffroy and renewing his acquaintance with Clemenceau, they too often came to Giverny. Geffroy's presence was invariably soothing, as Monet respected him not only as a friend but as a critic. Monet's regard for other critics was not high. He had over the years made a collection of newspaper cuttings, which included most of the articles in which his painting had been derided, condemned and vilified. "One never hears so much nonsense talked, as about a picture," Monet would say, quoting Jules de Goncourt.

There were also visits from the excitable but irresistible Octave Mirbeau who had rented the Château de la Madeleine, not far from Vernon. When unable to visit, Mirbeau would write. Being somewhat insomniac, he was a prolific writer of letters, not all of which were sent. Like Monet, he was anxious and moody. He, too, would inveigh against the weather and became emotional at the sight of his garden spoilt, as often happened in Normandy, by the rain and wind. Mirbeau's letters contained such extravagant exhortations as this: "...Yes, Monet, let us love something so as not to die or go mad! But I think that such advice is not for us, for if ever we do go mad it'll be from loving too many things."

The established ritual of Giverny was soon to be interrupted by an invasion. It came about in the simplest way, the result of a few coincidences and a little enthusiastic gossip. An American painter, Theodore Robinson, who had been painting in the Fontainebleau region and was associated with the Barbizon school, had been introduced to Monet by his friend Deconchy. Robinson liked Giverny and came back to live and work there.

Shortly after, another American, Metcalf, a student at the Académie Julian, walking in the neighbourhood, discovered Giverny by chance in apple blossom time. He was enchanted, and went to the village *epicerie-buvette*, the general store-cum-bar, to ask for a room. Mme Baudy, the proprietress, unable to understand English was so alarmed by the long haired, bearded stranger that she slammed the door in his face; but he returned several weeks later with two friends, made his wishes understood and they were given lodgings. Learning that Monet lived close by, they called on him, and, contrary to all expectations, were politely invited in. Monet, who was in a good humour that day, was delighted to talk to them and asked them to lunch. In the days to come, these pioneers of the American invasion were often made welcome at Monet's home. On this occasion they spent the afternoon painting with Blanche. When they went back to Paris, Metcalf and his friends talked too much. The legend of Monet had gradually reached the art academies, and the secret of his hiding place had been discovered. Exaggerated rumours spread about the village at the foot of the hills, where the food was good and the price was reasonable. The rush began.

Gradually, all over the place, skylights were inserted in the brown roofs and no less than forty studios appeared in a village whose original population was three hundred. Every street had its painter, its sculptor, even its writer. The Belgian painter Théo van Rysselberghe settled in the rue du Milieu, William Hart in the rue du Colombier, while in the rue du Pressoir, a Miss Wheeler set up a painting school for American girls—'peintresses', the locals called them.

It was something unprecedented in Giverny's history. Americans predominated; but there was also a Czech, Radinsky, who was crazy about cycling and skating and who eventually married his model. There was a Norwegian, Thornley, an Englishman, Watson, a Scot, Dice—a turbulent fellow who wore a kilt and played the bagpipes—and even a Japanese, assistant to the American sculptor MacMonnies. Many of them had been brought by Robinson or by Sargent: Hart, Beckwith and Theodore Butler, for example. The Johnstones had come from America; they had bought a house, and so had the Finns, the Perrys, Hart Frieseke, Rose and many others. They had heard about Giverny, they had come to see it for themselves and they had stayed—for a few hours, a few weeks, a few years or a lifetime.

Two huge studios had been installed in the top floor of the *epicerie-buvette*, and another built in the garden. It had now become the 'Hôtel Baudy' where one could dance and drink till all hours. The dining-room walls were covered with paintings, some of them gifts, others left as pledges for unpaid bills.

Dice, finding the tea undrinkable, had taught Madame Baudy the art of making tea and how to prepare Welsh rarebit. The village store now sold tea imported from England, puddings, maple syrup, marshmallows, and even paintbrushes, canvases and frames, for Madame Baudy had become agent for Foinet, the famous Parisian purveyor of artists' materials.

The excitement which had overtaken the once peaceful village distressed Monet. Constantly harrassed by young painters seeking lessons or advice he was finally forced to shut his doors to all but a select few. These included Robinson, Beckwith and Theodore Butler, a friend of Sargent's. Occasionally Monet would visit the Perrys, his American neighbours where he would smoke and chat with Mrs Lila Cabot Perry, herself a painter, whom he often invited to his studio. The first time she went there she was impressed by the painting Monet had just begun, a portrait of Suzanne in a deep mauve, almost violet dress, leaning on a table with her face close to a bunch of sunflowers; the treatment was as surprising as the colours, which were unusually dark for Monet, and much lower in key. The purpose of her visit was to purchase, at a friend's request, a painting from her famous neighbour. Having chosen an Etretat landscape, she was surprised to be told that she could not take it away. The sky and clouds needed retouching, declared Monet, he would have to return to Etretat to recapture the exact light effect that he wished to convey.

Mrs Perry described another event concerning Monet's cherished hothouse. A new heating system had been installed and, deeply concerned about his tropical plants, Monet decided to stay up all night to ensure that the system functioned properly, since any shortcoming might cause irrevocable damage to his orchids. Alice, failing to dissuade him from such action, decided to join him. When informed of this the girls were alarmed at their parents spending all night alone in the hothouse and decided to keep them company. The whole family stayed there till morning, watching over a heater which, predictably, functioned most satisfactorily.

Though distressing for Monet the invasion of Giverny meant that there was much more entertainment for the children. Every day painting went on busily in the studios and in the fields, where white umbrellas opened out like mushrooms. Models were imported specially from Paris or were pretty peasant girls from the district. The Perry daughters and the

Hoschedé sisters, meanwhile, were having great fun with Watson and his wife, who, by way of riposte to a satirical journal published in Paris, *Le courrier français*, were preparing one of their own at Giverny. *Le courrier innocent*, published locally by the most primitive methods and copiously illustrated by their friends.

Michel and Jean-Pierre were accompanied on their botanical trips by Metcalf, who collected birds' eggs. There were shooting parties with Rose, reputedly the best shot in Giverny; there were bicycle rides with Radinsky; and photography with Robinson.

Some of the artists gave up painting. One went so far as to start a chicken farm at the Ferme de la Côte. And Stanton Young, a painter and a redoubtable tennis player, who had often partnered the King of Sweden at Cannes, set aside his brushes to organise a couple of tennis courts at the Hôtel Baudy. Monet, who excelled at the game, never went there; but an endless succession of matches took place, watched from the terrace of the hotel by a crowd of spectators.

In the evenings there were parties. The village people mingled with models, painters and 'peintresses', and came for drinks to Baudy's bar where Dice played the bagpipes and Radinsky the piano, and someone else the banjo, while dancing went on into the night.

More sedate and exclusive entertainments were held in certain houses, in an atmosphere redolent of the southern states of America. Elsewhere hospitality was less formal. Young gave a momorable party for 150 Americans from both Paris and Giverny at the Moulin des Chenevières; others, like Borgord, kept open house.

Monet disliked social gatherings and kept well away from these rowdy parties. His only public appearances in Giverny were at the fêtes held on ice. At the first signs of frost Jean-Pierre, the family champion, would set off to investigate. When he announced that the ice was firm the sledges and skates were dragged out and the season began. There were races and competitions by day, and fêtes by night, illuminated by hundreds of paper lanterns. In the clear winter nights shadowy figures darted and twirled and sledges were sent speeding forward amid shouts and laughter. The spectacle drew crowds from all around. On Christmas Eve the fête ended with midnight mass, and was resumed after the service with supper parties in private houses, where jugs of cider, almond cakes and foie-gras toast awaited the skaters.

A visitor to the Hotel Baudy

In November 1894 the Hôtel Baudy welcomed its most famous guest, Paul Cézanne, who had come to see Monet and to paint at Giverny. Monet was pleased to give support to Cézanne. They exchanged paintings, lunched and drank together and it was on this visit that Monet introduced him to Clemenceau, Geffroy and Rodin. Cézanne, shy and unpredictable, was somewhat wary of meeting strangers but warmed instantly to Geffroy, and they subsequently became close friends. Clemenceau, too, charmed the painter with his energy and wit. On the day of his meeting with them Cézanne behaved very oddly. He wanted to be decorated, because he thought this meant recognition and success and he was anxious to be taken seriously at last. Rodin had been awarded the Legion of Honour, and the sight of his ribbon impressed Cézanne so much that he drew Mirbeau and Geffroy to one side and remarked: "Monsieur Rodin isn't at all proud, he shook hands with me! A man who's been decorated." After lunch they all went for a stroll round the garden before visiting Monet's studio; suddenly, in the middle of the main walk, Cézanne knelt down before Rodin and thanked him for shaking hands with him. His fellow guests were amazed.

At the Hôtel Baudy Cézanne inevitably attracted some attention. Mary Cassatt, the American Impressionist painter, who was also staying at the hotel at that time commented thus:

> Monsieur Cézanne is from Provence and is like the man from the Midi
> whom Daudet describes: "When first I saw him I thought he looked like a
> cut-throat with large red eyeballs standing out from his head in a most
> ferocious manner, a rather fierce looking pointed beard, quite grey, and an
> excited way of talking that positively made the dishes rattle." I found later
> that I had misjudged his appearance, for far from being fierce and

cut-throat, he had the gentlest manner possible, 'comme un enfant', as he would say. His manners at first rather startled me—he scrapes his soup plate, then lifts it and pours the remaining drops in his spoon: he even takes his chop in his fingers and pulls the meat from the bone. . . . . Yet in spite of the total disregard of the dictionary of manners, he shows a politeness towards us which no other man here would have shown. He will not allow Louise to serve him before us in the usual order of succession at the table; he is even deferential to that stupid maid, and he pulls off the old tam-o-shanter, which he wears to protect his bald head, when he enters the room. Cézanne is one of the most liberal artists I have ever seen. He prefaces every remark with: 'Pour moi' it is so and so, but he grants that everyone may be as honest and as true to nature from their convictions; he doesn't believe that everyone should see alike.

Then one day while dining at Monet's with Renoir and Sisley (who had been invited especially to celebrate Cézanne's visit) he abruptly left the table and did not return. His friends had been commenting favourably on his work, but Cézanne, thinking they were making fun of him, could bear it no longer. All his paintings were left behind at the inn, but Monet collected them together and forwarded them on. In due course he received a letter from Cézanne full of regret, but quite failing to explain the reason for his behaviour. They were never to meet again.

A complex family

When Monet and the Hoschedés settled at Giverny they put aside memories of earlier backgrounds and Giverny became their base. Home was now the unpretentious Maison du Pressoir, although only Michel and Jean-Pierre had grown up there. Camille Monet and Ernest Hoschedé belonged to the past. They appeared in paintings by Manet, Renoir and Monet—scenes at Argenteuil and Montgeron—that hung in the studio drawing-room and bedrooms of Le Pressoir, but their names were seldom mentioned, and questions concerning them were avoided.

Hoschedé had remained in correspondence with his family from Brussels and eventually returned to Paris. He had been legally exonerated from his business failure and now intended to take up new interests in Paris. He had been able to take a few of his paintings to Brussels, and thus had enough capital on his return to set up a number of magazines. He also edited an annual volume on the official Salon. An exceptionally charming and generous spirited man, he was at once welcomed back by his old Parisian friends, and subsequently resumed his activities in artistic circles.

It was evident that a reunion with his wife and children was impossible; although they maintained an intermittent correspondence his visits to the children were few and far between, but birthday and Christmas greetings were exchanged regularly. When Ernest Hoschedé died in 1891 his funeral took place at Giverny in the presence of the whole family. Then a new chapter in this complex story began.

Monet was now uncontested head of the family. For a long time everyone, Alice included, had addressed him as 'Monet' and used the familiar 'tu': everyone, that is, except Jean-Pierre and Michel, who for some strange reason were embarrassed and always spoke to him in the third person, addressing him as 'il' or 'on'. They would say: 'on va au marais?' meaning, 'Father (or Monet), are you going to the marsh?' It was easier in letters, where they called him 'Papa Monet'; his replies were signed affectionately, 'your old father', or 'your old Monet who loves you as his child'.

But when the formal 'Chère Madame' gave place to 'my dear Alice', difficulties arose. It had taken considerable courage for pious Mme Hoschedé to brave public opinion when, deserted by her husband, she had gone to live with a man whom she could not marry. Monet, moreover, was not religious. For all their great mutual tolerance, this unconventional relationship disturbed them in different ways: lacking social sanction, it embarrassed Monet, who was traditionalist and conservative in such matters; lacking God's sanction, it made Alice unhappy. Divorce was not part of their code; somehow it smacked of sin, and the idea of it never even occurred to her. As for Monet, who smiled at Cézanne for putting on his Sunday best to go to Mass, and who, although he entertained the curé to lunch, would never enter a church except for unavoidable ceremonies, he would not have dreamed of acting counter to other people's convictions.

Alice's relatives, the Raingo family sanctioned the relationship. They held Monet in great esteem and admired his work as an artist, and Alice's sisters, Cecile, Marie, Isabelle and Marguerite frequently visited their sister at Giverny. On the other hand Monet's brother, with whom he was later to quarrel irrevocably, had for a long time only consented to receive him alone or accompanied by his two sons, since he was deeply concerned about the opinions of provincial society.

Until their father's death no pressure had been put on the children to consider a career, and they had been presented with no responsibilities. Now, however, Monet undertook to see to their future, and this was a somewhat disturbing prospect.

The patriarch's sway was undisputed; Monet's word was law and there was simply no question of a marriage without his approval nor a career which he thought unsuitable. In this respect he was a typical 'haut bourgeois' father.

Jean Monet studied chemistry in Switzerland and practised in Rouen with his uncle. When he married Blanche Hoschedé in 1897 he became both stepson and son-in-law to Alice, Blanche both stepdaughter and daughter-in-law to Monet: and what made it still more confusing for other people (since as far as the family was concerned it was all quite straightforward) Monet often spoke of Blanche as 'my daughter'. Outsiders were always making mistakes about the two Madame Monets, Alice and Blanche. Blanche meanwhile continued painting and was to become Monet's devoted companion and housekeeper after Jean's premature death in 1914.

Jacques, whom Manet had painted at Montgeron as the *Child with flowers*, and whom Monet visited in Norway took up his career in shipbuilding and married a Norwegian, Inga Jorgensoen, the widow of a Bergen lawyer who already had a small daughter, Anna Bergman.

Germaine and Pierre Sisley were planning to marry. The two families had visited each other frequently throughout their childhood, but it was a match of which Monet did not approve. Pierre Sisley was an inventor, an occupation which Monet thought very insecure. Quite firmly, he forbade the marriage and Germaine had little choice but to acquiesce in his decision. Broken-hearted and unhappy, nothing seemed to distract her, despite the concerts, and dinners at Marguery's in Paris to which Monet took her. Finally he sent her off, in the winter of 1901, to Saint-Jean-Cap-Ferrat to stay with the Deconchys urging her to enjoy herself. Here she met their friend, Albert Salerou, a lawyer from Monaco and a great collector of books and butterflies. By this time Pierre Sisley's image had faded. Germaine and Albert Salerou married at Giverny on the 12th November 1902 and settled at Cagnes, near Renoir. Later they moved to Paris when her husband, drawn towards politics, went to work with Clemenceau.

Jean-Pierre and Michel, having completed their *Flora* with Abbé Toussaint, were also amateur inventors. Only one of their inventions had the slightest practical utility, a bicycle built for two which had a certain local success. Then Jean-Pierre studied agriculture in Perigord. He stayed with a friend of Alice's and finally married her daughter, Geneviève Costadau in 1903. Michel, though he cherished a lifelong passion for mechanical things, had no career. He, of all the children, seemed the least able to cope with his father's domination, and was moody and reserved. He refused to put his name to the *Flora*, and was a clandestine painter, overawed, no doubt, by his father's image. Only after his father's death did he marry Gabrielle Bonaventure, an artists' model of whom Monet greatly disapproved. They later took part in one of the first expeditions to cross the Sahara.

During this time Suzanne Hoschedé formed an attachment with the young American painter, Theodore Butler. Both Alice and Monet initially viewed the match with some reserve. They knew little about this young friend of Sargent's except that he was something of a trend-setter among Americans in Paris. They were anxious lest Butler should want to take Suzanne off to America.

Alice wrote to Butler's mother in Columbus and further enquiries were made through Monet's American friend, Beckwith. It was learnt that the Butlers were a family of prosperous and irreproachable financiers who had played an important part at the time of Lafayette in the American struggle for independence. Monet and Alice were relieved at this news and the wedding was agreed.

The date, however, was constantly being changed despite the fact that Courtland, Theodore's brother, had come to France for the celebration. Preparations threw the Monet household into chaos. Courtland, who had business in London, declared that if the date of the ceremony was not fixed when he returned, he would go back to the United States.

Everything had been dealt with, including administrative details, yet something very strange seemed to be brewing in this normally well organised household. Mme Hoschedé was in a state of quite exceptional agitation. Monet made cryptic remarks, and Suzanne was in tears. Then, to his great astonishment, Theodore Butler received the following letter from Suzanne:

> My dear Butler . . . . I can quite understand your being sad at the date of our wedding not being fixed yet; but I promise you that Maman will do her very best to make things right for me and that it will be soon. Only what you don't know is that another very serious matter is going to be decided shortly, and this is worrying Maman. So you mustn't mind if she is sometimes preoccupied and less gracious than usual. Monsieur Monet wants to marry Maman and in order for things to be done properly, they are both very anxious for it to happen before our wedding, so that Monsieur Monet can take my father's place and give me away in church, and also that his position with regard to our family may be easier. This is a great secret I'm telling you; you must swear not to breathe a word of it to anyone.

Suzanne's wedding took place on the 20th of July 1892 and the festivities went on until late into the night. The event was celebrated with great rejoicings, and all the sportsmen of the village fired the customary volley in honour of the couple as they left the Mairie, after which Suzanne was led to the altar by her stepfather. The whole village and all the artist colony turned up for the celebrations.

Four days earlier a much quieter ceremony had taken place. It was the wedding of Claude Monet and Alice Raingo Hoschedé in the presence only of their witnesses. Eight years later after Suzanne's death in 1899 Theodore Butler was to marry her sister Marthe.

Monet at home

The efficient running of the household, over which Alice presided, involved a number of servants. The kitchen was run by Rita or Caroline, and the laundry by Delphine with the assistance of her daughter, Denise, who from her earliest childhood was fascinated by Monet's pleated jabots. Breuil and Lebret were in charge of the gardens, while Fouillard was chauffeur, later succeeded by Sylvain, who was equally skilled as mechanic or driver, at stretching a canvas on its frame or at bottling wine. In his spare time he also played the hunting horn like his forebears, huntsmen from the Sologne.

The life style of the household became increasingly simple and informal. The master of the house was always referred to as 'Monet', never 'Monsieur'. Menus were never written down nor dishes decorated. There were few reminders of material wealth, only some Florentine pieces of furniture and the precious samovar for tea. There were just two dinner services, one for everyday, dark blue imitation Japanese, and another yellow set, made to Monet's order to match the dining-room walls.

Alice supervised the well stocked larder, prepared menus a week ahead and kept note of her guests' tastes. Her correspondence and Monet's took up a good part of the day; like many women of her time she kept a journal.

In the summer holidays the house and garden were invaded by a host of children and grandchildren: Jim, Lily, Anna, Sisi and Nitou, together with their various friends—Julie Manet, Pierre and Jeanne Sisley, Paule Gobillard and her sister (the future Madame Paul Valéry), the young Pissarros, particularly Lucien—a favourite of Monet's, Jean Renoir and a swarm of cousins. During the summer they would go for evening walks, particularly to the pond where on the 6th June Monet's saint's day was celebrated with a display of fireworks.

In winter, with fewer guests, Alice and Monet would spend their evenings reading: the *Memoirs* of Saint-Simon, Tolstoy, Ibsen, Maeterlinck, Balzac, Flaubert or the Goncourts. Monet's favourite bedside book was the *Journal* of Delacroix.

Perhaps the household's most basic concern was good food. Anyone who did not share this interest was held to be a barbarian. Monet, however, was not a great connoisseur of wine, although he particularly liked Sancerre and other light Loire vintages, a dry fragrant rosé or a full bodied red wine from a modest vineyard in the Massif Central.

Monet supplemented his kitchen garden by buying the Maison Bleue in the rue du Chêne, which had a walled garden as large as that of Le Pressoir. New fruit trees were planted and a resident gardener was put in charge of forcing the plants, of the special herb garden and of the mushroom bed in the cellar. The more fragile plants were protected by forcing frames, for Monet thought the local produce somewhat limited and so he cultivated many of the aromatic herbs and vegetables of the South.

Monet was a gourmet. At table, he always carved himself and dressed the salad, showering it with black pepper. He liked asparagus very lightly cooked, and cèpes laid in layers with fresh garlic, covered with olive oil, then cooked in the oven. He would cut off the wings of a roast duck and sprinkle them with nutmeg, kitchen salt and pepper, and he would then send them back to the kitchen to be grilled until they were piping hot. He liked his foie gras from Alsace, his truffles from Perigord, and beans cooked in wine from Chanturne. He was interested in all sorts of recipes and would try out dishes that he had sampled elsewhere or simply imagined, and required the kitchen to adapt and invent as they went along.

After a succession of undistinguished cooks came the difficult reigns of Caroline, Rita and then Melanie. Next came Marguerite. As a young kitchen maid she had learnt her job under Melanie, an excellent cook, adding her own incomparable skill to the cunning of her teacher. When she married, Monet was so averse to losing her that he engaged her husband Paul as butler.

Marguerite officiated amidst a battery of saucepans, fish kettles, moulds of every shape and size and various stoves. In the kitchen with its blue tiled walls, on which hung rows of glittering copper pans, she bustled about between her marble mortar, her chopping board, the preserving pans and the indispensable scales.

Marguerite was adept at marinades and sauces and could give the simplest dish a special flavour. She was especially good with vegetables which were invariably picked at dawn from the kitchen gardens of Le Pressoir or the Maison Bleue. She was equally skilled at preparing American dishes when Theodore Butler was invited, an elaborate menu for a distinguished visitor, or *la crème somptueuse* for Clemenceau, the simplicity of whose tastes amazed her. Tea making was one of the few culinary tasks that she did not perform. The precious caddy was kept out of her reach, in the glass-fronted cabinet in the studio drawing-room. Paul would bring in the boiling water and, of course, the meringues, cheese straws and lemon madeleines made by Marguerite. Her pastries were particularly popular with family and guests; when asked the secret of her success she would shrug her shoulders. She knew by the look and feel when the dough was right.

Marguerite in her spare time studied the family cookery book, but invariably disagreed with the experts on some point or another. The unquestionable fact was that when Marguerite finally abdicated the kitchen, things were never the same.

Monet and the motor car

For the Monet household, the tragic event of the last year of the century was the death of Suzanne. She contracted paralysis soon after the birth of her daughter, Lily, and her condition deteriorated so rapidly during the next five years that Jim, her son, was entrusted to his Monet grandparents and brought up by Marthe (who later became his stepmother). Sisley had died at the beginning of 1899. Monet and Alice stayed on in Paris for a while after the funeral. On returning to Giverny they found Suzanne very weak and tired. That night, the 6th of February, 1899, she died in her sleep.

Alice gave way to despair and to an almost unnatural grief. Every morning at dawn she visited the cemetery; if Monet was away she would write incoherent letters which brought him instantly back to Giverny. He bought Alice a portrait of Suzanne painted by Henner in the old days at Montgeron. He also took her to London; but Alice remained inconsolable, and her depression cast a gloom over the entire house. A fortunate distraction was provided by the project for alterations to the lily pond, to which the villagers objected since it might involve the diversion of the Ru. Then came the suggestion of a motor car. The boys, particularly Jean, Michel and Jean-Pierre, had shown great excitement over the first motor shows with their dazzling displays of the inventions of Amedée Bollée, de Dion-Bouton, Renault and Delamare-Debouteville. There were steam-driven, gas-driven and electric cars, vehicles of every size and shape.

Monet, a townsman turned country dweller, had never owned a carriage nor ridden a horse, neither could he ride a bicycle. But in 1901, urged on by the children and hoping it might be a diversion for the grief stricken Alice, he ordered a Panhard-Levassor, which arrived while he was in London at work on the *Thames* series of paintings.

Monet did not drive himself, so he used Fouillard as a chauffeur, who was succeeded three years later by Sylvain, who held the post for thirty-two years. Monet had not been mistaken: Alice adored speed and was always the first to suggest a drive. Alice with a party of children would sit in the back of the open car with caps and goggles, wrapped in long fur cloaks. Sometimes they would set out just for the ride, sometimes to take Monet to one of his painting sites. When a second Panhard-Levassor appeared in the garage, followed by Jean-Pierre's Hotchkiss and Michel's Donnet-Zedel the whole family would go off in convoy for picnics, carrying chairs and a great hamper full of cold meats and pies, cakes and a selection of wines. They watched speed races at Gaillon and saw the competitors in the Paris-Madrid race driving through Beauce. Welcoming any pretext for an excursion, they visited Jean and Blanche in Rouen, the Butlers holidaying at the seaside at Yport, Veules-les-Roses and Pourville; they drove to Caudebec-en-Caux to see the equinoctial tidal wave sweeping across the lower Seine; and one mealtime a heated argument sent them off to Lamotte-Beuvron, beyond Orléans, to taste the famous upside-down apple pie of the Tatin sisters. Then, in October 1904 there was a drive to Spain after Monet impulsively announced his desire to see Velasquez's work in the Prado. He and Alice, together with Fouillard, promptly set off to Madrid for three weeks. Monet was at last able to see the paintings of Velasquez which he had thought about for so long; then he hurried back to finish his paintings in London. Later the faithful 937 YZ was replaced by a limousine for Monet, while the second Panhard made way for the 'Zebra', a small van which was used for shopping.

Visiting Monet

An invitation from Monet was a rare privilege, a true mark of his friendship, accorded only to a few besides those who had been his companions in the early days of struggle.

The entertainment at Giverny was simple: an invitation to lunch, a walk round the garden, a visit to the hothouse and the studios, a glimpse of the artist's private collection of paintings. And the same guests were invariably to be seen sitting in the wicker armchairs of the studio drawing room, strolling down the garden paths, taking photographs or examining the pond.

In 1897 an annexe was built beside the linden trees. The ground floor provided the gardeners' room and later the garage and a dark room for photography. On the floor above, beside the new apartments prepared for Jacques and Inga, as well as Jean and Blanche, Monet had a studio made. It was a large, well-lit room, which on the south side gave on to a glazed gallery overlooking the hothouse.

Here Monet spent the winter finishing the work begun during the summer and completing paintings which he only signed at the last moment. On the walls hung paintings of every period, irrespective of chronology, on which he continued to work. Others were stacked, awaiting a visit from Durand-Ruel, the Bernheim brothers or some other collector. It was a sparsely furnished room, containing only a glass cabinet full of Japanese ceramics and a roll top desk on which stood a photograph of a Manet self-portrait, next to a few

The Garden

The drawing on the following two pages shows the positions of the principal plants in Claude Monet's garden as listed below by seasons.

Spring.

Yellow winter jasmine on the wall close to the gate. Maple sycamore tree. Snow-drops. White Christmas roses. Primulas. Mauve and violet Irises germanica. Pink Peonies.

Border of Aubrietias. Snow-drops. White Christmas roses. Primulas. Mauve and violet Irises germanica. Pink Peonies.

Border of Aubrietias. Primulas. Pansies. Viola cornuta. Irises germanica.

Border of Aubrietias. Primulas. Pansies. Viola cornuta. Snow-drops.

Border of Aubrietias. Crocus. Jonquils. Viola cornuta. Irises germanica.

Snow-drops. Christmas roses. Primulas. Jonquils. Syringas. Viburnums.

Border of Aubrietias. Snow-drops. Jonquils. Tulips.

Border of Aubrietias. Snow-drops. Jonquils. Tulips.

Border of Aubrietias. Snow-drops. Jonquils. Tulips.

Border of Aubrietias. Snow-drops. Jonquils. Tulips.

Lime trees. Snow-drops. Primulas.

Border of Irises germanica. Jonquils. Tulips.

Border of Irises germanica. Jonquils. Tulips.

Metre wide borders of Irises germanica. Dutch Irises. Oriental poppies. Peonies. Pansies. Doronics. Columbines. Primulas.

Border of Irises germanica. Tulips.

Irises germanica.

Border of Irises germanica. Jonquils.

About 12 square places of 1.50m. by 1.50m. in the green with border of Irises germanica. Jonquils. Peonies. Japanese cherry trees. Japanese apple trees. Japanese maple trees. Oriental poppies.

Border of Irises germanica. Jonquils.

20. Border of Aubrietias. Jonquils. Tulips ordered by colours (red, yellow, pink, rose and parrot tulips). Columbines.

21. Green. Horse chestnut trees.

22. Border of Irises germanica. Doronics.

23. Border of Irises germanica. Doronics.

24. Border of Irises germanica. Doronics.

25. Border of Aubrietias. Jonquils. Clematis. Leopard's banes. Tulips ordered by colours (red, rose, pink, yellow, parrot tulips).

26. Jonquils. Columbines.

27. Jonquils. Columbines.

28. Pond.

29. Irises germanica.

30. Border of Aubrietias. Jonquils. Pansies.

31. Irises germanica.

32. Border of Irises germanica. Doronics.

33. Border of Aubrietias. Clematis.

Summer and autumn.

1. Japanese anemones (white and pink). Cactus Dahlias. Maple sycamore tree.

2. Japanese anemones (white and pink). Mauve Asters. Border of Campanula carpatica. Passion flower climbing on the wall of the central heating. Dahlias (yellow, white and pink).

3. Border of Campanula carpatica. Climbing roses and rose trees with simple flowers (pink, yellow, orange). Rudbeckias. Virginia creeper on the house.

4. **Border of Campanula carpatica. Rose trees and Climbing roses with simple flowers (pink and red). Clematis. Sages. Virginia creeper on the gouse.**

5. **Border of Campanula carpatica. Climbing roses. Pot marigolds. Aconitums. Pinks.**

6. Japanese anemones (white and pink).

7. Border of pinks. Red Pelargoniums. Cannas. Sages.

8. **Border of pinks. Red Pelargoniums. Cannas. Sages.**

9. Border of Campanula carpatica. Red Pelargoniums. Pinks.

10. Rose trees with red flowers. Pelargoniums. Sages. Japanese anemones. Clematis. Morning glories.

11. St. John's worts. Lime trees.

12. Climbing Roses. Clematis. Morning glories. Snapdragons. Cactus Dahlias with simple flowers.

13. Climbing Roses. Clematis. Morning glories. Snapdragons. Cactus Dahlias with simple flowers.

14. Creeping Nasturtiums. Climbing Roses with simple rose and crimson flowers. Sunflowers. Cone flowers. Daisies. Asters (white, pink, violet). Delphiniums. Bellflowers. Cactus Dahlias.

15. Climbing Roses. Asters. Sunflowers. Foxgloves.

16. Delphiniums Cone flowers. Daisies.

17. Morning glories. Clematis. Japanese anemones. Snapdragons. Bellflowers.

18. Japanese anemones. Asters. Cactus Dahlias.

19. Climbing roses with simple flowers. Asters. Cactus Dahlias.

20. Border of pinks. Evening primroses. Daisies with white flowers. Heliopsis. Willowherbs. Snapdragons. Delphiniums. Mulleins. Pot marigolds. Cone flowers. Gladiolus by colours. Cactus Dahlias.

21. Green. Horse chestnut trees.

22. Japanese anemones. Nasturtiums climbing on the enclosure along the road. Pot marigolds. Bellflowers. Mulleins.

23. Japanese anemones. Nasturtiums climbing on the enclosure along the road. Pot marigolds. Bellflowers. Mulleins.

24. Japanese anemones. Summer clematis. Snapdragons. Asters. Pot marigolds.

25. Snapdragons. Daisies. Pinks. Bellflowers. Summer clematis. Cactus Dahlias. Dead man's fingers.

26. Lilies. Gladiolus. Foxgloves. Monkshoods.

27. Foxgloves. Monkshoods. Blue thistles.

28. Pond. 2 Sumacs close to the pond.

29. Japanese anemones. Pinks.

30. Pinks. Monkshoods.

31. Japanese anemones. Snapdragons.

32. Japanese anemones. Nasturtiums climbing on the enclosure along the road. Bell flowers.

33. Sweet peas. Golden rods.

34. Blue Hydrangeas. A maple sycamore tree in the grass.

The lily pond garden.

1. Japanese quince tree. (Spring).

2. Raspberry bush with flowers. (Spring).

3. Bamboos.

4. Bamboos.

5. Petasites.

6. Weeping willow.

7. Black bamboos.

8. Wisteria. (Late spring).

9. Japanese cherry tree. (Late spring).

10. Alder tree.

11. Ash tree.

12. Willow.

13. Peony bush. (Late spring).

14. Japanese apple tree. (Spring).

15. Azaleas. (Spring).

16. Rhododendron. (Spring and summer).

17. Poplar.

18. Fern.

19. Ginkgo.

20. Barberry.

21. Rose tree. (Summer).

22. Lilies. (Summer).

23. Solomon's seal.

24. Pampas grass.

25. Irises. (Spring).

26. Water lilies. (Summer).

27. Holly tree.

28. African lily. (Summer).

29. Tamarisk. (Spring).

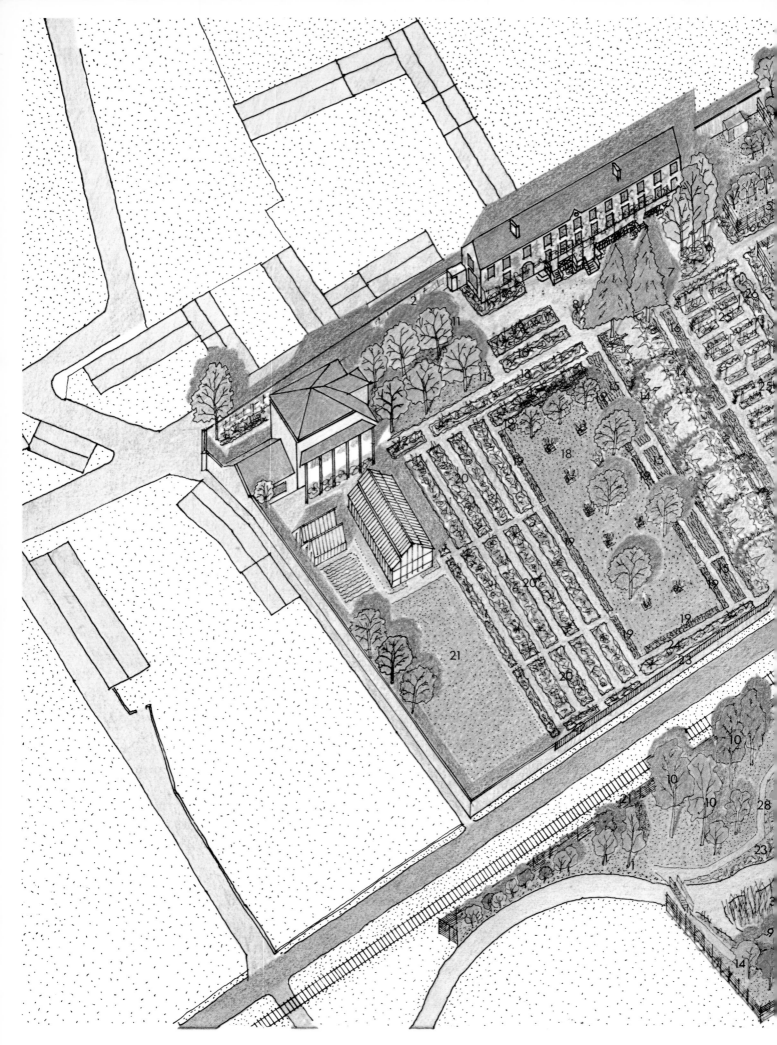

personal treasures, including a letter from Mallarmé, yellowing with age and addressed thus:

> 'Monsieur Monet que l'hiver ni
> L'été sa vision ne leurre
> Habite en peignant Giverny
> Sis auprès de Vernon, dans l'Eure'.
> Stéphane Mallarmé

> (Monsieur Monet, whose vision deceives him neither
> in winter nor summer, lives, painting, at Giverny near Vernon, in the Eure).

After visiting the studios Monet would take his guests up the short flight of steps, through the wide French windows and into the house. The bareness of the rooms was startling, especially for a period when most interiors were over furnished, with fringed and tasseled hangings, fussy ornaments and heavy curtains. Here, there was not much furniture and most of it was painted. Rush mats and a few tiny oriental rugs on the floor scarcely muffled one's footsteps, the only luxury being the wealth of paintings and Japanese prints on the walls.

On the staircase leading to Monet and Alice's suite of rooms hung a Toulouse-Lautrec poster of Yvette Guilbert, a *kakemono* and a reproduction of a Hogarth print. Monet had hung Cézanne's *Negro* in the bathroom and in the two bedrooms he kept a Corot, four Jongkinds, three Delacroix, a Fantin-Latour, a Degas, two Caillebottes, three Pissarros, a Sisley, twelve Cézannes, nine Renoirs, five Morisots, a watercolour by Chéret and two by Signac, a pastel of Vuillard's and two Rodin bronzes.

The studio drawing-room, simply furnished with wicker armchairs and chintz covered sofas, held a collection of Monet's own paintings—representative of every period, hung side by side in three rows. There were pictures once left as pledges which he had been able to redeem or exchange, and others which he had refused to part with or which had fortunately remained unsold, such as the *Sunrise at Vétheuil* which Faure, the operatic singer, had rejected because there was not enough paint on the canvas. These paintings retraced the story of his life, disclosed his meticulous exploration of light and the play of light on water, on stone, on snow or forest, in his many journeys—to Christiania or Venice, Bordighera or London, Etretat or Antibes, the rugged coast of Brittany or the soft skies over Holland. Each picture brought back memories and anecdotes of his travels.

Monet's pottery collection and the prints hanging on the stair-well that led to the second studio, and in the mauve drawing-room which served as his library, revealed his interest in Japanese art. He even owned sketchbooks by Utamaro and Hokusai.

The dining-room, ceiling and furniture included, was entirely painted in two shades of yellow. Prints by Hiroshige, Hurulolu, Utamaro and Hokusai framed in plain wood were carefully arranged and hung by Monet. Here, Monet entertained Rodin, Sargent, Durand-Ruel and his family, Geffroy, Natanson, Ajalbert, the Kurokis and other Japanese friends, visitors from London and Paris, and those who had settled outside Paris such as Mirbeau, Sacha Guitry and his actress wife Charlotte Lyses. Paul Valéry and the Bernheims came occasionally, and Clemenceau constantly.

Table talk was about food and wine and the fortunes of the garden; little about politics, even less about painting. In the summer the french windows were wide open and following some rustic tradition the insects were kept at bay by hanging tomato leaves on the walls. During these meals on the balcony Monet always sat facing the garden, looking straight down the main walk, so as to lose no detail of the play of light on his flower beds.

Such moments of relaxation were the time for reminiscences. Monet rarely spoke of his childhood and adolescence in Le Havre, for he had but few pleasant memories of that period of his life. The only relative he held in affection was his Aunt Lecadre, who had done a little painting herself. Although puzzled by her nephew's pictures, she had given him support and hospitality, and had presented him with a small painting by Daubigny that he had always admired.

Monet never passed judgment on people, he only implied his opinion of them by his tone of voice. He would speak of the difficult periods in his life calmly and without regret. He talked about Manet, about Frédéric Bazille, who was Jean's godfather, and about the colourful crowds and strange animals he had seen in Algeria: he would tell of the evenings spent at the Brasserie des Martyrs, bringing vividly to life the excitement of those days of struggle and partisanship. Here he had met all the Bohemian world of Paris, artists of every calibre, good and bad. Here for the first time he had seen Courbet, without daring to approach him; Courbet the magnificent, who later lent him money as he lent it to everyone, and who kept open house in the rue Hautefeuille for a hungry crowd. Imitating Courbet's strong Franc-Comtois accent, Monet described how one day at Le Havre the pair of them decided to call on Dumas, whom neither of them knew. The landlady raised some objection about introducing them; but Courbet cut her short saying: "Tell him it's the Master of Ornans." The two men made friends immediately and Dumas invited Courbet and 'the young man', as he called Monet, to lunch with him next day at La Belle Ernestine's restaurant at Saint-Jouin. On the way there, Dumas poured forth his reminiscences to the amazement of a silent Monet. Courbet was talkative and racy, Dumas witty and eloquent. They subsequently spent many days together at Le Havre, singing and cooking! Much later, in 1916, Monet revisited La Belle Ernestine's with some friends. Ernestine, who was by then very old and far less beautiful, showed them the carefully preserved telegram sent her by Dumas thirty-eight years previously, bidding her keep 'force crevettes', plenty of prawns, for his guests.

Monet's garden

"I perhaps owe having become a painter to flowers", said Monet in 1924. Monet created a garden wherever he settled; at Argenteuil, at Vétheuil and finally at Giverny. He told one of his visitors to Giverny:

> "My garden is a slow work, pursued with love and I do not deny that I am
> proud of it. Forty years ago, when I established myself here, there was
> nothing but a farmhouse and a poor orchard . . . . I bought the house and
> little by little I enlarged and organised it . . . . I dug, planted, weeded
> myself; in the evenings the children watered."

Only the yews and limes survived from the original orchard. Cherry trees and japonicas had replaced fruit trees, and a fence on which nasturtiums and roses had been trained to climb added to the wall. By dint of constant care and enrichment at vast expense, the inhospitable soil was finally mastered. Until 1892 Monet had worked the garden himself, with the children's help; eventually it became so full of flowers that he could no longer cope. Now Monet had a head gardener recommended by Mirbeau, with five under-gardeners, one of whom was exclusively employed looking after the pond, keeping down the weeds and tending the water lilies. Monet gave daily orders, inspecting the garden several times a day. No detail escaped him; he would correct a vista, recompose a clump of flowers, alter a pattern, and he insisted on the removal of fading blooms. He planned his flower beds according to the principles that governed his palette, with light colours predominating and monochrome masses in juxtaposition. Very little soil was left bare in the garden; no flowers of a fancy variety, no coloured or variegated foliage were allowed, and he was particularly fond of briar roses and of star-shaped dahlias with tubular petals.

The daily discussions with Felix Breuil, the head gardener sometimes became heated arguments. Breuil was concerned with the quality of the soil, the spacing of plants, the need to clip and prune, but Monet, although aware of these necessities was chiefly concerned with the relationships of colour density and texture. There was a constant succession of flowers from early spring onwards; they carpeted the ground, growing in clusters, in masses, in cascades; there were bowers of roses and arches of clematis, and creepers everywhere clasping the trunks of trees.

Although the layout of the flower-bed had a geometric basis, there was none of the formality of the typical French garden. Rectangles and straight lines disappeared under the spreading mats of nasturtium, wild geranium, aubrietia and pink saxifrage. It was a painter's garden, where everything followed a certain rhythm, the supple tall stems of iris, lilies, foxgloves alternating with the wild plumes of grasses and the bold masses of poppies and eschscholtzias; where harmonies of tawny yellow, crimson and gold, saffron and blue were contrasted. Every item in the garden was designed to play a part; even the straight furrows in the raked gravel of the paths were not a chance effect.

The plan that underlaid this apparent confusion was in keeping with the nature of the land, taking advantage of its slightest rise and fall and the alternations of sun and shadow, and allowing scope for the spread of self-sown species.

As early as January the garden was bright with yellow jasmine, Christmas roses, snowdrops and scillas, which heralded the spring crocuses, the first primroses and the successive waves of tulips and narcissi. Monet would eagerly watch the young shoots thrusting up through the dormant earth, and if he longed for a more exuberant spectacle he had only to visit his hothouse; in that moist luminous place the many varieties of orchids gave out a heady scent. Hanging roots interlaced overhead, mingling with the fragrance of the luxuriant miniature jungle of sensitive plants, ficus and parasitic ferns clinging to the bare mossy stems of dwarf trees. Glowing Korean chrysanthemums and the strange ruffled crests of strelitzias bloomed beside a small pool of frail African water lilies.

Monet's pond was opposite the main gate of Le Pressoir, over the chemin du Roy, across the railway line. As Clemenceau remarked, Monet had his own train! In 1893 Monet was able to satisfy his abiding passion for water by becoming the owner of a river. Just across the garden, in the meadow through which the river Ru flowed, there lay a tiny pond where wild water lilies and kingcups flourished. Monet bought it and planted the edges with every sort of aquatic plant that would grow in the Giverny climate. A system of sluices renewed its water from the river. Undisturbed by any current, frail water lilies, delicately coloured, floated on the still, sun warmed water. The bridge, a single arc without piers inspired by a Japanese print, spanned the two banks.

The pond, like the garden, was originally conceived for the delight of the eye, but gradually acquired greater importance as a subject for painting. Soon it began to appear as too small and symmetrical for the needs of the painter and Monet planned to divert the course of the Ru and to acquire another small plot of land. This would enable him to enlarge his water garden and alter its shape at will. There were endless arguments with the women who washed their linen in the Ru, and the peasants whose cattle grazed in the riverside meadows were afraid that the strange unfamiliar plants that were invading the water might poison their animals. The Parish Council deliberated, and with many reservations, finally gave permission for this branch of the Epte to be diverted.

Monet remodelled the little pond, enlarged it repeatedly, curved its edges as he pleased; with the help of twisting paths and clumps of trees he succeeded in producing an effect of considerable space. The Japanese bridge was now laden with white and mauve wisteria while close by was a forest of rustling bamboos, and thick on the bank of the pond were irises, meadowsweet and petasites. There was a profusion of roses—bush roses, standard roses and that bold rambler, *Belle Vichyssoise*, which climbed like a liana round the trunks of the trees. There were huge ferns and great clumps of rhododendrons and azaleas. Weeping willows leaned into the pond while on the water floated Monet's water lilies. When he created his lily pond Monet had not suspected that it would be an inexhaustible source of inspiration for over thirty years, and that up till his last days he would paint its every aspect, at every hour its shimmer and its reflections and the submerged vegetation seen through the transparent water. He was to work at hundreds of paintings and studies there, like the Japanese artist who never tired, throughout his life, of painting the same garden. It was impossible to say where the gardener's work stopped and the painter's began, for the two were manifestly interconnected.

Clemenceau and the Nymphéas

Alice died on the 19th of May, 1911. Monet's friends gathered around to pay their last respects to a kind friend and hostess. Even Degas, now a blind old man feeling his way with a stick, came to Giverny.

Monet was broken by Alice's death. For some time he was indifferent to the things that had previously concerned him so deeply. He deserted his studio, and for days at a time he would not set foot in the garden. Each morning he would be found by Marthe, who now shared the running of the household with Geneviève, re-reading or destroying Alice's letters. He ignored his correspondence, which Marthe dealt with, only writing wild, despairing letters to friends and children.

In the Autumn, to everyone's great relief he took up painting again. ". . . Winter is coming and I couldn't bear to remain inactive during these dreary days," he wrote to Durand-Ruel. "I shall first try to finish some of my paintings of Venice . . ." He had not the heart to go back to Venice to revise his work on the spot, as he had always done in the past, when he would only finish a picture after correcting his studies at the place and at the season at which they had first been sketched. When the exhibition of his paintings of Venice opened in 1912, Monet told Durand-Ruel in bitter disappointment:

> ". . . . More than ever today, I realise how artificial is the undeserved fame I have won. I keep hoping to do better, but age and sorrow have drained my strength. I know beforehand that you'll say my pictures are perfect. I know that when they are shown they will be much admired, but I don't care because I know they are bad. I'm certain of it. Thank you for your comforting words, your friendship and all the trouble you have taken. I hope to see you next Sunday for lunch as usual. . . ."

Monet had given up all thought of long painting trips, and when he began to work again he became almost a recluse. He discouraged guests at Giverny and would rarely leave the house and garden. He went occasionally to Paris for a concert or a dinner, where he would meet Vuillard, Roussel or Chéret. It was at this period, too, that he made the acquaintance of Bonnard, who had come to live at Vernonnet nearby, and whose friendship played a special part in the last years of his life. Somewhat later, when he undertook the *Décoration des Nymphéas* (The Water Lily Decorations) he had several visits from Matisse.

Monet had more or less deserted Brouant's restaurant, where there was always a place kept for him at the table reserved for the Goncourt Academy. During this dark period there were a few lighter moments: in 1913 the American singer Marguerite Namara insisted on singing for Monet beside the pond. This involved the not inconsiderable feat of transporting Theodore Butler's piano from the rue du Colombier to the water garden. The recital over, Monet posed beside her for a photograph by Sacha Guitry.

Meanwhile the greatest possible disaster for a painter threatened Monet. In 1908 he was troubled with failing eyesight, but continued working. In 1912 he finally visited an eye specialist in Paris who diagnosed a double cataract and recommended an operation. Monet refused, fearing that an operation would radically alter his vision.

Increasingly taciturn and depressed, Monet was helped through this difficult period by Clemenceau, whose attention increased the more his friend suffered from what Mirbeau called a "paralysing moral rheumatism." Clemenceau wrote letters, issued invitations, gave Monet a backgammon set, and after endless arguments persuaded the painter to consider travelling in order to shake off his melancholy. Accompanied by Michel, Jim and Lily, Monet set off for Lucerne, St. Moritz and Davos. Long walks and the discovery of an unfamiliar landscape enchanted and refreshed him.

The year 1914 brought fresh ordeals to Monet, even apart from the outbreak of war. On the 10th February Jean Monet died at Giverny aged forty-seven. For some time he had been suffering from a nervous disease which affected his mind. At times silent and withdrawn, at other times incoherent and rambling, he showed little awareness of reality. It was a harrowing time for Blanche and Monet and one which left Monet as depressed and gloomy as he had ever been.

Blanche thenceforth became Monet's housekeeper and companion, a difficult and often thankless task, of which Monet was sometimes aware. "How kind she is, and how maddening I must be to everyone," he confessed once. Monet went through every stage of discouragement and when behaving abominably he was unapproachable. Blanche, often in tears, would be forced to inform the kitchen of his latest whim—he wanted this, or didn't want that or had decided to eat no lunch at all.

Sometimes their spirits would revive. Blanche invariably accompanied Monet to his painting site, carrying his equipment as of old; she would change the canvas on his easel as the light altered, and then get back to her work. And in the evenings after dinner they could be seen happily playing backgammon together.

But for Blanche's patient support and Clemenceau's endless encouragement it is doubtful if the ageing Monet would have survived these difficult years. Clemenceau, writing directly to Blanche, to whom he referred as "Monet's blue angel," would give her support too: ". . . . Since our dauber is working well, let's do him the favour of letting him keep at it. When he has something to say, we shall be there to listen. In the meantime, keep him shut up. Love to both of you."

The war was soon to isolate Blanche and Monet at Giverny and brought many fresh anxieties for both of them. Friends and family were scattered, and Monet waited anxiously for news of them. The Butlers were safe in America, but Michel, Jean-Pierre and Albert Salerou had all been called up as had Renoir's sons, Pierre and Jean, and Michel Clemenceau.

Monet and Blanche waited for the post, listened to communiqués and at night heard the cannon thundering from Beauvais; meanwhile stretcher-bearers went past in an endless stream along the chemin du Roy, bringing the wounded from the front. Monet followed the army's movements on a map and was resolved, at all cost, not to leave Giverny, although at one stage he considered putting his collection in safety. Clemenceau, as Prime Minister during part of the war, often called at Giverny, accompanied by some high government official with whom he discussed affairs of state on the journey so as to waste no time. He kept Monet well informed, commenting on events and communiqués.

Meanwhile Monet had done very little painting. Again it was Clemenceau who came to the rescue, firing Monet with a new purpose in life. He pursuaded the painter to take up a project which he had often considered and always abandoned; to paint a series of mural sized water landscapes. For this project he had to construct a third studio, 39×75 feet large and 49 feet high. This studio was not completed until 1916, for there was great difficulty in finding labour as all men of military age were under arms. Monet was in despair at the ugliness of the building, and felt somewhat ashamed at having allowed so hideous a thing to be built. He had always been the first to protest indignantly about buildings that disfigure their natural surroundings.

A huge skylight and a system of awnings through which the light could be filtered as he wished, provided the artist with the means to recreate the luminous atmosphere of the lily pond. He thus began work on his series of the *Décoration des Nymphéas* which he intended to present to the State. These paintings occupied Monet for the next ten years and represented the culmination of his life's work; the concrete realisation of some thirty years of research. Unfortunately they were to entail a great many administrative problems and endless hesitations on Monet's part, and in the end were not to be inaugurated until 1927. They almost brought about a quarrel between Clemenceau and Monet. For a long time indeed there had been no written contract for the donation, which depended solely upon a verbal agreement between the two friends. Clemenceau for his part went to infinite trouble to get offcial consent to all the conditions demanded by Monet.

The rooms in the Orangerie were rearranged at great expense. Monet had asked for elliptical rooms for the display of his nineteen panels. He had his way down to the slightest details. The bequest was signed at Vernon by Monet and Paul Leon, director of the Beaux-Arts, in April 1922. Clemenceau had successfully carried through the negoti-ations and was delighted. But again he reckoned without Monet's hesitations; the painter repeatedly decided that his task was beyond his powers. Sometimes he wanted to destroy the whole thing, sometimes he would repaint the almost completed panels, and Clemenceau, who paid regular visits to keep an eye on things, was appalled to see how the development of Monet's cataract had gradually and very seriously altered his vision. Instead of re-touching the panels effectively, he was in constant danger of ruining them. A day came when, feeling overwhelmed, Monet thought of destroying his work and starting all over again. Then, finally, of abandoning the project and giving part or the whole of his collection to the State by way of compensation. He wrote to Clemenceau, who became very angry. It had been hard enough securing a postponement for the delivery of the panels, and now

Monet was going back on his word! Clemenceau told him indignantly that there could be no if's and but's when one has made a promise, that enormous sums of money had been spent on his behalf and that, however discouraged he might feel there could be no question of not keeping his word. As usual, counting on Blanche to influence Monet, he wrote to her:

Paris, 7 January 1926.

My dear friend,
I have received a shocking letter from Monet and I won't stand for it. By this same post he will get my answer, which you will probably find very harsh, but which is absolutely sincere.

If he does not alter his decision I will never see him again. . . .

G. Clemenceau

The argument produced the desired effect. Blanche did her utmost, and between them she and Clemenceau made Monet see reason.

In the meantime his operation for a cataract had meant a considerable waste of time for Monet. The panels he had painted before and after raised certain problems. Here again it had taken all Clemenceau's influence and all Blanche's patience to persuade him to have the operation, and to help him through it.

Clemenceau had introduced Monet to Dr Coutela who eventually operated on his right eye. Monet was an unspeakably difficult invalid, but Clemenceau and Blanche were untiring in their devotion and Michel, also, showed great consideration. The doctor kept them informed by letter. Blanche visited Monet's bedside all the time he was in hospital and Clemenceau kept in constant touch. He wrote to Blanche:

. . . . The doctor tells me he has severed the small membrane from the iris. He was only afraid lest the patient might vomit, which would have interfered with the operation. This is probably why it took longer than I should have expected; anyhow it's done now: that's the chief thing. We shall see what the doctor says in a few days. Please be kind enough to keep me informed. I can't say any more just now. I have sent a wire to Monet, and I shall reply to Coutela asking for a further note after he has visited you today. He gives me a good report of the patient's state of nerves. So we may hope for the best.

My love to my old brother [Monet], my roundabout little sister [Blanche], not forgetting the baby [Michel].

G. Clemenceau

Monet's last days

The war had driven away the cheerful American residents of Giverny. However, many of them kept their houses and visited intermittently from 1918 to the financial crisis of 1929. Other regular visitors had succeeded them, more writers than painters; Hart's house had long since become a boarding house where actors stayed. Finally the village had been discovered by the Surrealists, who flocked to stay with Teddy Toulgouat at weekends at the 'Ferme de la Dîme': Breton and Aragon, Michel Leyris, Drieu la Rochelle, Tristan Tzara and many others. Monet had gone on living apart from all this. Nobody had been able to persuade him to accept the Legion of Honour or a chair at the Institut. It is doubtful whether he was aware of the vast changes taking place in the world around him.

Family life was little altered. The Butlers had at last come back from America and their return had been celebrated with a grand family dinner and Monet made gifts of his paintings. Yet most of Monet's friends had died: Renoir, Durand-Ruel, Rodin, Degas, Mirbeau: at home, he lost Marthe in 1925. Gradually age deprived Monet's step of its briskness. At the time of his cataract he exchanged his customary felt hat for a broad-brimmed panama to keep the light from his eyes. He still chain-smoked Caporal cigarettes, though he never finished them. He lost his staunch countryman's figure and his increasing thinness betrayed the onset of a fatal illness.

By the beginning of 1926 he was showing ever more frequent signs of fatigue. Clemenceau was at first not seriously alarmed, assuming that his friend was simply suffering from old age. A resolute optimist, despite his own exhaustion, he came as often as possible to keep Monet company and to raise the spirit of the old painter.

When Clemenceau was at Giverny Monet recovered his appetite a little. If he had not been outside for several days, Clemenceau would keep him in the garden for an hour or more. Eventually the facts had to be faced: the doctors diagnosed pulmonary sclerosis, to which long years of smoking must have contributed. Only one lung was functioning, and that not well. He was ordered to rest, but Clemenceau objected that this would lower his morale and accelerate the progress of the disease, and was convinced it would be better to stimulate him.

Monet's two doctors gave contradictory opinions. One forecast that a violent haemorrhage would kill him, the other considered he might linger on for a long time. Monet never suspected the nature of his illness and was always ready to receive visitors. He cheered up when friends were present, and seemed to recover some of his old zest. He started painting once more and although he was determined not to touch the *Nymphéas* again, he could not face being parted from them. He wanted to look at them again at leisure. Knowing how brief a time he had left Clemenceau had the tact not to agitate for their dispatch to the Orangerie.

As the garden broke into its full glory it became apparent that the end was near and throughout the summer Monet grew thinner and weaker. He was much affected by the death of Geffroy on the 6th of May and he had little appetite for food. Two weddings, Lily's and Sisi's were the last festivities he enjoyed. The summer days were spent dreaming on the bench beside the lily pond or painting whenever he was able. Blanche and Michel were constantly by his side and Bonnard came to see him a fortnight before his death.

By October Monet was in considerable pain and very weak. Clemenceau found that he had lost all interest in painting and could talk only of the garden and of the lily bulbs that the Kurokis were sending from Japan. At the end of November the pain seemed to cease but thereafter he sank rapidly. On the morning of December 5th Clemenceau was sent for and towards midday Monet died.

Monet was given the quiet funeral he had always wanted. At Jean-Pierre's request the prefect made no speech. Clemenceau was waiting at the graveyard. Monet's body was taken from the house which still spoke of his presence and away from his garden, now lying numb under the first winter frosts. He was carried to his grave in the old village hearse, accompanied by his family, a crowd of silent villagers and a few friends. Clemenceau, Bonnard, Roussel and Vuillard were pall-bearers. There was no religious ceremony and no funeral oration. There were only flowers, his friends and his family.

The Arrival

Collection Piguet

Alice Hoschedé and three of her
daughters in the spruce-tree walk,
in front of the brick-dust coloured
house.
Collection Toulgouat

Mme Alice Hoschedé
Collection Toulgouat

Jean-Pierre Hoschedé and Michel
Monet, on their arrival at
Giverny.
Collection Toulgouat

The Artist's Garden at
Vetheuil. 1880.

amille Monet in the
rden, Argenteuil. 1876.

47

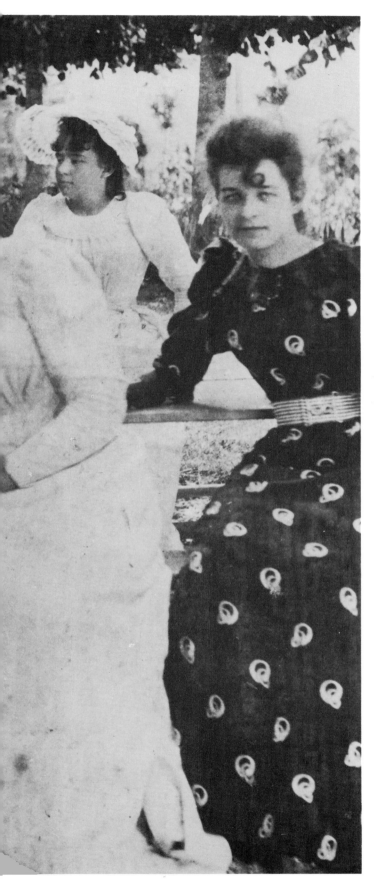

The Monet Family *ca* 1886

1 Claude Monet.
2 Alice Hoschedé.
3 Jean-Pierre Hoschedé.
4 Michel Monet, younger son of the painter.
5 Blanche Hoschedé, married to Jean Monet in 1897.
6 Jean Monet, elder son of the painter.
7 Jacques Hoschedé.
8 Marthe Hoschedé.
9 Germaine Hoschedé.
10 Suzanne Hoschedé.

A few years after the arrival at Giverny; a family group under the lime-trees, one summer afternoon.
Collection Toulgouat

49

Another way of capturing the fleeting moment; here we see Monet about to photograph the water-lilies, his figure reflected in the pond which, originally intended as pure ornament, was to provide him with inexhaustible subjects through the ever-changing play of light on water.
Collection Piguet

On the balcony where they lunched in summer; Monet and three of his step-daughters, Suzanne, Germaine and Blanche Hoschedé. As was common at that period, the three sisters were dressed alike. Notice, at the foot of the balcony, the flowerpots which had accompanied the Monet-Hoschedé family throughout all their ordeals.
Collection Piguet

The orchid hothouse overlooked
by the second studio, built in 1897
with new rooms for the children,
several of whom were now
married.
Collection Toulgouat

The Garden Develops

Poppy Field Near Giverny.
1885.

he Pink Boat. 1885.

lanche Monet Painting.
. 1885–90.

The house, with its walls still bare standing at the foot of the hills, before it the huge, gently sloping orchard of which Monet was to make a luxuriant garden rich in surprising colour harmonies.
Collection Piguet

Monet in late winter, on the look-out for signs of spring.
Collection Toulgouat

Monet visited his gardens several times a day. As he walked about, the thought of painting was constantly in his mind, and the successive transformations of his lily pond resulted from these lengthy meditations. Here he is seen beside one of the sluices which allowed fresh water from the Ru to replenish the pond. *Collection Toulgouat*

Landscape With Haystack.
1891.

Poplars on the Epte. 1890.

anch of the Seine Near
verny. 1897.

1893. Under the lime trees: a visit from Paul Durand-Ruel, the art dealer and patron of the Impressionists, a close friend of the family. Durand-Ruel, wearing a bowler hat, is seen talking to Monet and Madame Suzanne Hoschedé-Butler. Seated, far right, Alice Hoschedé, now Madame Claude Monet.
Collection Piguet

The house in winter with the glassed-in "studio-drawing room", his first studio.
Collection Piguet

Opposite the house, in a lush meadow through which the Ru flowed between willows and poplars, lay a small pond in which common water-lilies and wild irises grew. Monet enlarged and remodelled this and planted it with more exotic lilies and every sort of aquatic plant. On the bridge, the shape of which was inspired by a Japanese print hanging in the dining-room, we see Monet with Anna Bergman, a Norwegian girl who married one of Monet's stepsons.

Collection Toulgouat

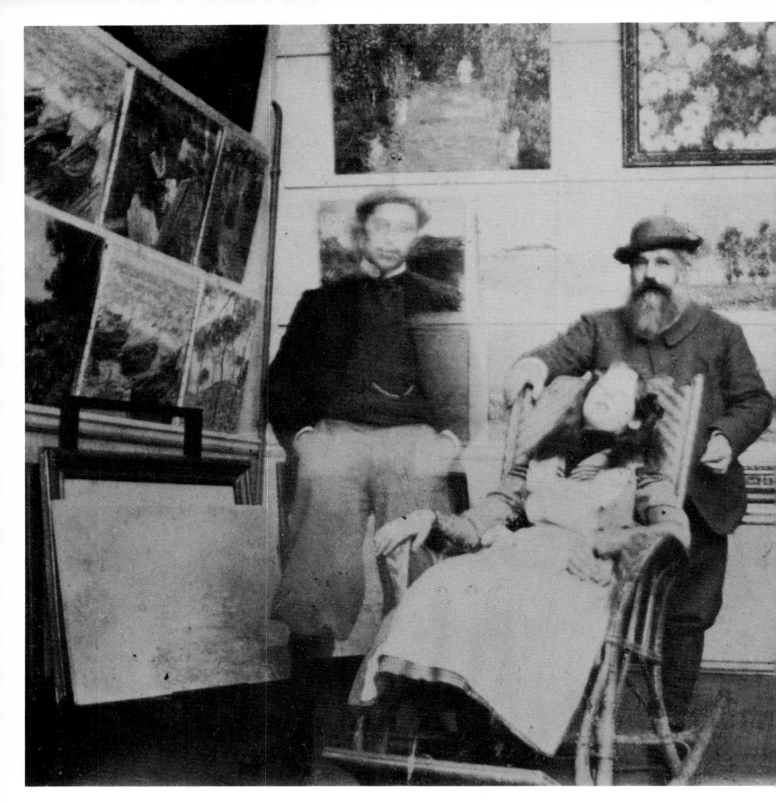

In the second studio, where
visitors were sometimes entertained, Monet is seen rocking
Anna Bergman's chair; beside
them is Michel Monet, the
painter's younger son. Paintings of
different periods were hung on the
walls, regardless of chronology.
Collection Toulgouat

Monet's Expeditions

Collection Toulgouat

The Garden, Giverny. 1895.

The Garden at Giverny.
1900.

Autumn 1908. The last "painting
trip". Monet and Alice were
staying with J. S. Sargent at the
Palazzo Barbaro. The inevitable
photograph with pigeons in the
Piazza San Marco.
Collection Piguet

Monet, who never drove himself,
with Butler, waiting for their
chauffeur, Sylvain.
Collection Toulgouat

May 1907. A family expedition to
Lamotte Beuvron by car: a
pilgrimage to the hotel of the
Tatin sisters, creators of the famous
upsidedown apple pie. Monet and
Lily Butler on the steps of the
hotel.
Collection Toulgouat

ly 1905. A trip along the
ormandy coast by motor car:
onet, Blanche Hoschedé-Monet
d Marthe Hoschedé-Butler.
llection Piguet

Left to right: Lily Butler, Jim
Butler, Blanche Hoschedé-Monet,
Marthe Hoschedé-Butler,
Madame Alice Monet, Claude
Monet.

Collection Toulgouat

In Monet's library, also known as the "mauve drawing-room", its walls hung with Japanese prints: Jim Butler sitting with his toys on a sofa. He was then living with his Monet grandparents, his mother Suzanne having become paralysed. For four years, accompanied by Alice and Marthe, he visited her daily in the nearby Rue du Colombier.
Collection Toulgouat

Monet yields to pressure from the photographer, Lily Butler.
Collection Toulgouat

1910. During the floods which had seriously damaged the gardens, Monet and his step-granddaughter Lily Butler walk about Giverny in the snow with mingled anxiety and delight.
Collection Toulgouat

Monet, although a restless character and a domestic tyrant, could also be a cheerful and lively companion.
Collection Durand-Ruel

Monet and his wife beside the lily pond one afternoon.
Collection Piguet

December 1908. On their way
k from Venice, Monet and his
e stayed for a few days at
gnes with Germaine Hoschedé
l her daughter, Sisi, standing to
right of her mother. Germaine
schedé had married Albert
arou, a lawyer from Monaco.
ey took the opportunity to visit
Renoirs, who were already
ng at Les Collettes.
lection Toulgouat

31 October 1900: Theodore Butler
married, as his second wife
Marthe, the eldest Hoschedé girl,
who was to bring up Jim and Lily.
Suzanne Hoschedé Butler had
died at Giverny on 6 February
1899, a few days after the death
of Sisley.
Collection Toulgouat

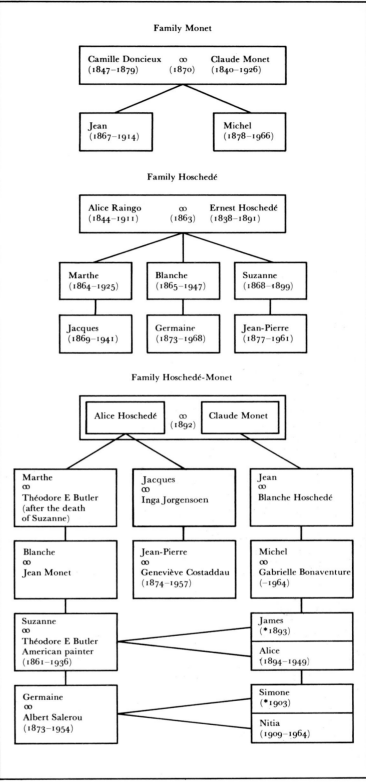

Family Monet

Camille Doncieux (1847–1879) ∞ (1870) Claude Monet (1840–1926)

- Jean (1867–1914)
- Michel (1878–1966)

Family Hoschedé

Alice Raingo (1844–1911) ∞ (1863) Ernest Hoschedé (1838–1891)

- Marthe (1864–1925)
- Blanche (1865–1947)
- Suzanne (1868–1899)

- Jacques (1869–1941)
- Germaine (1873–1968)
- Jean-Pierre (1877–1961)

Family Hoschedé-Monet

Alice Hoschedé ∞ (1892) Claude Monet

- Marthe ∞ Théodore E Butler (after the death of Suzanne)
- Jacques ∞ Inga Jorgensoen
- Jean ∞ Blanche Hoschedé

- Blanche ∞ Jean Monet
- Jean-Pierre ∞ Geneviève Costaddau (1874–1957)
- Michel ∞ Gabrielle Bonaventure (–1964)

- Suzanne ∞ Théodore E Butler American painter (1861–1936)
- James (*1893)
- Alice (1894–1949)

- Germaine ∞ Albert Salerou (1873–1954)
- Simone (*1903)
- Nitia (1909–1964)

1. Paul Durand-Ruel.
2. Ernest Vialatte.
3. Isabelle Pagny.
4. Joseph Pagny.
5. Anna Bergman.
6. Mme Alice Claude Monet.
7. Jean Monet.
8. Claude Monet.
9. Marthe Hoschedé Butler.
10. Theodore Earl Butler.
11. Jean Pierre Hoschedé.
12. Madeleine Pagny.
13. Blanche Hoschedé Monet.
14. Jeanne Sisley.
15. Fernand Haunddorf.
16. Alice Raingo-Pelouse.
17. Lucien Raingo-Pelouse.
18. Achille Pagny.
19. Alice Butler.
20. Suzanne Raingo.
21. Germaine Hoschedé.
22. Pierre Sisley.
23. James P. Butler.
24. Germain Raingo-Pelouse.
25. Inga Jorgensoen Hoschedé.
26. Mr l'Abbé Toussaint curé de Giverny.

The Garden. 1902.

ater Lilies. 1899.

Monet studies his lily pond from
the Japanese bridge, which in
Summer was covered with a
profusion of wisteria.
Collection Sirot

Monet at Home

Collection Madame Verneiges

In front of the second studio, broad beds of irises of a single colour.
Collection Piguet

One had to pick one's way carefully along the main walk to avoid treading on the freely-trailing nasturtiums.
Collection Toulgouat

82

...hower of clematis and a cloak
...irginia creeper and climbing
...es on the walls of the house.
...lection Piguet

Flower garden beside the third
studio.
Collection Truffaut

The photographer Nadar, who
had lent his studio for the first
Impressionist exhibition in 1874,
had become a close friend of
Monet's and often photographed
him and his family.
Collections Piguet and Toulgouat

Monet in a characteristic pose, in his country clothes, with the inevitable cigarette between his fingers.

Collection Sirot
Photograph Bulloz

In the dining-room with its painted furniture, the choicest dishes were served in a setting of sober simplicity. On the walls, which were painted in two shades of yellow, Japanese prints were set out in an arrangement designed by Monet himself. The guests who met here regularly included Clemenceau, Rodin, Mirbeau, Geffroy, Paul Durand-Ruel, Sacha Guitry and John Sargent, Sisley, Pissarro, Renoir and even the eccentric Cézanne.
Collection Piguet

Water Lilies. 1904.

e first studio had become a
ting-room where the family
egathered and wrote their
ers; Monet sat here when he
s not painting, and here were
ng specimen pictures from

every stage of his career.
Collection Piguet

The Japanese Garden. 1910.

llow and White Water
lies. *ca.* 1920.

Winter in the leafless orchard, with no trace of vegetation excep[t] in the hothouse, where orchids, strelitzias and tropical ferns wer[e] grown.
Collection Piguet

In Summer, climbing roses, clematis and virginia creeper covered the trelliswork around t[he] house.
Collection Truffaut

Opposite: 1913. Monet showing the pond to the American singe[r] Namara, who absolutely insiste[d] on singing to him; Butler had t[o] move his piano over from the R[ue] du Colombier.
Collection Piguet

The Lily Pond

The Pond after the initial work
enlargement had begun. On the
newly built bridge, Michel Monet
and Anna Bergman.
Collection Piguet

The aquatic plants introduced by
Monet, although visible, had not
yet spread to the banks nor
attained the desired effect of
profusion.
Collection Piguet

The Pond, further widened, where
lilies grew in abundance.
Collection Toulgouat

By deepening the curve of the pond and cunningly arranging the clumps of grasses and groups of trees, Monet had succeeded in giving the impression of wide vistas in a limited space. The area of the water garden was not more than 8,000 square metres.
Collection Piguet

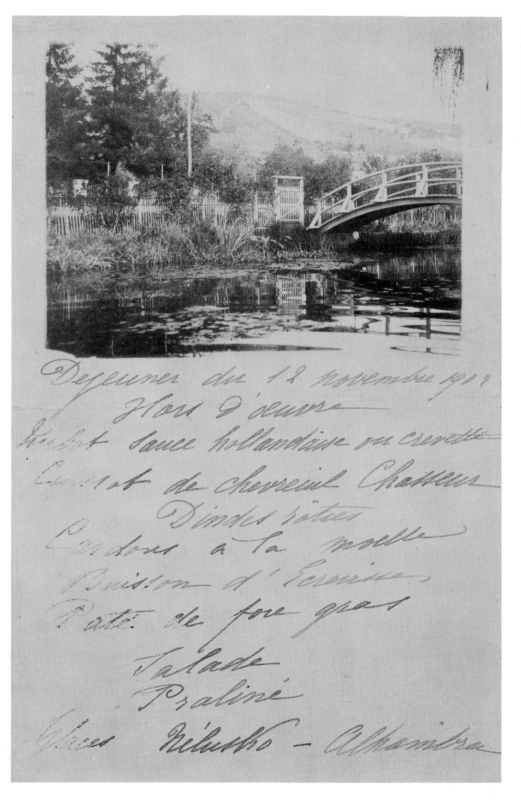

12 November 1902: Menu of the
wedding breakfast for Monet's
youngest step-daughter, Germaine
Hoschedé, on her marriage at
Giverny to Albert Salarou. The
couple subsequently settled at
Cagnes, close to Les Collettes
where Renoir was living.
Collection Piguet

Winter 1910: the lily pond and
part of the garden were
submerged, and floods prevented
the little train from running, and
killed a great many plants. It was
a long time before the damaged
areas recovered their original
appearance.
Collection Toulgouat

Above, top photograph
Theodore Butler, Jim Butler,
Monet and William Hart walking
round the pond.
Collection Toulgouat

Above, bottom photograph
Monet, Theodore Butler, William
Hart, Jim Butler, Alice Monet.
Collection Toulgouat

e Japanese bridge with its
hed framework, to which clung
te and lilac wisteria from
na and Japan. Monet with
nche Hoschedé-Monet, his
ddaughter and daughter-in-
, and his step-granddaughter
Salerou.
ection Piguet

the distance, on the bank, the
ch where Monet sat to gaze at
water-garden or think about
nting.
lection Toulgouat

e exotic lushness of the garden;
the left, the boat used by the
n whose sole task was to look
r the water-garden.
lection Piguet

99

The ritual walk to the water-garden and lily pond. On this occasion the guests were two Japanese friends and art collectors: M. Kuroki and his wife (neé Princess Matsukata), Clemenceau and Lily Butler, newly back from the U.S.A. All were passionate garden-lovers, and the Kurokis often sent Monet tree-peonies and the bulbs of certain lilies which were uncommon even in Japan and quite unknown in France. The route taken after lunch was invariably down the main walk, across the Chemin du Roy and over a steep ridge along which the little railway ran, to reach the lily pond. It was in June 1921, when the water-lilies were in full bloom. M. Kuroki undertook to be photographer; on the last picture, bottom right, can be seen Blanche Hoschedé-Monet, Michel Monet, Monet, Madame Kuroki, Clemenceau and Lily Butler.
Collections Piguet and Toulgouat

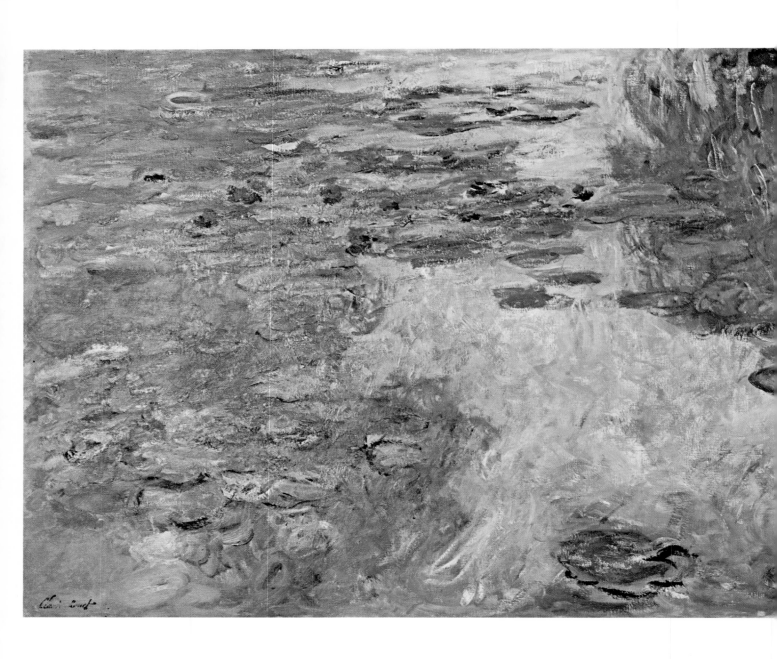

Water Lilies.

Water Lilies.

Many Japanese were early collectors of Impressionist paintings. Monet refused to let them have the *Decorations des Nympheas*, which he intended for the Orangerie. Here we see Mme Kuroki (who had just bought a painting at Giverny, entitled *Houses in the Snow*) and beside her Monet, Blanche Hoschedé-Monet, Lilia Salerou and Germaine Hoschedé-Salerou.
Collection Piguet

Monet beside the Minister of Fine Arts with, far right, Geffroy the art critic and friend of Monet and Clemenceau, and Paul Leon, an academician.

Opposite: June 1921. On the Japanese bridge: Clemenceau, Monet and Lily Butler.
Collection Toulgouat

The Garden, Giverny.

Irises by the Pond.
ca. 1920–24

Collection Piguet

Constantly cleared of the weeds and duckweed that spread all too rapidly, the pond with its still surface warmed by the sun's rays enabled the most delicate as well as the commonest sorts of water-lilies to flourish. Some were of African origin. They lay on the peaceful water in a wide range of colours from white to violet, including pink, yellow, red and mauve.

Décorations des Nymphéas

Collection Durand-Ruel

Monet in the third studio, known as the Big Studio, specially built for him to paint the *Décorations des Nymphéas* which he wanted to give to the nation, to be re-mounted in elliptically shaped rooms of the Orangerie in the Tuileries gardens. Begun in 1914, this studio was not completed until 1916; it was hard to find labour, since all available men were in the army. Finally the Big Studio was inaugurated by members of the Academie Goncourt after a lunch given by Monet.
Collection Piguet

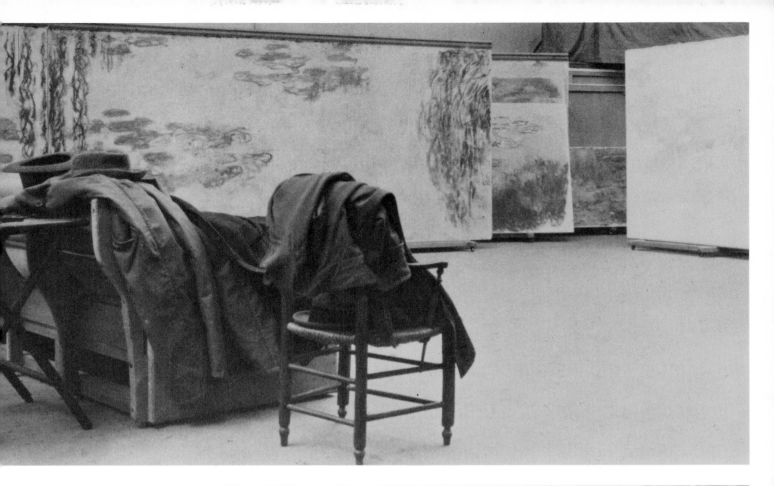

the Big Studio, hats and coats
by visitors who had come to
the progress of the *Nymphéas*
els. Note the extra long easels
bling the panels to be moved
will and studied in the order in
ch they were to be set out in
Orangerie.
ection Toulgouat

der his big white parasol
net worked hard at his studies
water-lilies. Blanche was
stantly beside him, changing
canvases on his easel to catch
varying effects of light. In
t, Nitou Salerou.
ection Piguet

osite: Monet with Germaine
Blanche in the Big Studio. By
y of relaxation he sometimes
nted other subjects there.
ind, a large mirror used for
self-portraits; one of these,
a at the foot of one panel, was
troyed in a fit of anger.
ection Piguet

113

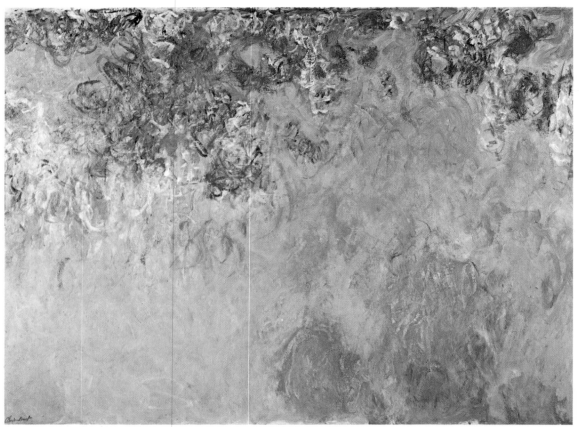

Wisteria

Water Lilies: Japanese
Bridge.

The Big Studio, practical becau
of its huge size—22 × 12 metres
seemed to Monet depressingly u
Horrified by the proportions of
this third studio, Monet wrote t
his stepson Jean-Pierre Hosched
who was then (19 August 1915)
the front: "... I am very well a
am working enormously hard. I
having a lot of trouble because
the uncertain weather we've be
having the last two months, and
shan't succeed in doing what I
wanted to, at any rate this year
I'm talking as though I had a
great many of them (i.e. years)
before me, which is just as crazy
as to have undertaken such a jo
at my age, and embarking on
gigantic constructions. It's mad
it's stark staring mad, particula
as it's horribly expensive. They'
gone and built me something
revolting, and I'm ashamed of
being responsible for it, when I'
always grumbling about the
people who uglify Giverny ..."
*Collections Durand-Ruel and
Piguet*

118

Monet's Garden

The famous horticulturalist
Georges Truffaut, a friend of
Monet's, admiring, with a
professional eye, Japanese peonies
in the water garden.
Collection Truffaut

The water garden in its full glory when shrubs, bamboos, irises, grasses, water-lilies and wisteria were all fully grown. The big willow that appears in the *Décorations*.
Collection Country Life

Beds of tulips and festoons of clematis in springtime.
Collection Truffaut

the head of the main walk, the
o original yew trees, partly
ling the house, whose walls are
npletely shrouded by the
ginia creeper that hangs like a
nopy over the balcony where
ich was eaten in summer.
lection Country Life

ery day the gardeners—there
re six of them—removed dead
wers. Monet kept a close watch
everything; he gave daily
tructions to the head gardener,
lix Breuil, who saw that they
re carried out and who
ntributed greatly to the beauty
the gardens. Breuil's father was
head gardener of Dr. Mirbeau,
her of Monet's friend the
ter.
llection Truffaut

Monet in front of his hybrid gladioli.

Collection Truffaut

A gravel walk leading to the lim
trees under which the family too
tea and spent summer afternoon

Collection Country Life

Enlargement of the pond allowed space for a wide variety of exotic water lilies.
Collection Country Life

The flower beds were laid out in geometric patterns crossed by intersecting pathways.
Collection Country Life

Water Lilies. Undated.

The Garden at Giverny,
Avenue of Rosebushes.
ca. 1924–25.

Willow trees near the sluice
between the pond and the Ru;
the lawn, clumps of pampas gra
Collection Truffaut

Irises near the Japanese bridge.
The small gate opened on to th
railway line, which had to be
crossed to reach the other garde
and the house.
Collection Truffaut

Opposite: Clumps of bamboos i
the water garden: the gardener
boat.
Collection Truffaut

Monet in his garden at the height of its summer splendour surrounded by borders of pinks, pelargoniums, cannas and sages. Original colour photograph appeared in *Illustration*. *Collection Durand-Ruel*

Varying moods of light and shade
enthralled Monet through the
changing seasons.
Collection Truffaut

Massed irises bordering both side of the pathway leading to the house.
Collection Truffaut

An aspect of the garden in late Autumn.
Collection Truffaut

26: Monet's last summer.

Haunted by the fear of losing his sight, Monet finally consented — with Clemenceau's encouragement — to an operation for cataract in 1923. After the operation, Monet rediscovered his garden and its true colours. He was to go on painting until two months before his death at midday on December 5th, 1926. *Collection Madame Verneiges*

The great round leaves of the
Petasites spreading over the
surface of the water.
Collection Truffaut

ew of part of the village; drawn
Monet's presence, a great
ny artists, mainly Americans,
led at Giverny. Skylights

appeared among the brown roofs
of farmhouses; there were some 40
studios in a village of 300 people.
Collection Country Life

Kalmia ferns and Japanese
azaleas.
Collection Truffaut

Index of Paintings

Monet: Chronology

1840

Monet and Rodin both born in Paris on November 14th. Monet's youth spent in Le Havre. Draws caricatures.

1858

Meets Boudin at whose suggestion he paints his first landscapes and outdoor subjects.

1859–1861

Leaves for Paris. Maintains correspondence with Boudin. Frequents the Brasserie des Martyrs where he saw Courbet for the first time but did not dare to speak to him. Works at the Académie Suisse where he meets Pissarro.

1861–1962

Military service in Algiers. Discharged from army for ill health. Meets Jongkind. Parental permission to return to Paris on condition he entered a studio and followed the teaching of the Ecole des Beaux-Arts. Enters Gleyre's studio where he meets Bazille, Renoir and Sisley.

1864

Meets Courbet. Leaves Gleyre to work at Chailly in the forest of Fontainebleau with Bazille, Renoir and Sisley.

1865

Shares Bazille's studio in Paris. Exhibits two paintings from Honfleur at the Salon. Paints le Déjeuner sur l'herbe.

1866

Success at the Salon with Camille, a portrait of his future wife Camille Doncieux.

1867

Women in the Garden rejected by the Salon. Birth of his son Jean. Great financial difficulties.

1868

Has only one painting accepted by the Salon. Financial problems worsen. Bazille's plans for an exhibition independent of the Salon abandoned for lack of money.

1869

Rejection at the Salon.

1870

Rejection at the Salon. Marriage with Camille. In England during the Franco-Prussian war, where he meets Daubigny, Paul Durand-Ruel and Pissarro who all enthusiastically study Turner and Constable. Bazille killed in action.

1871

Visits Holland and returns to France.

1872

Settles at Argenteuil where Renoir joins him.

1873

Meets his neighbour Caillebotte at Argenteuil. Inspired by Daubigny constructs a studio-boat.

1874

With the help of Pissarro Monet organises the first of the eight Impressionist exhibitions. Manet declines their invitation to participate, being more concerned with official recognition from the Salon.

1875

Works in Argenteuil. Camille Monet ill. Continuing financial difficultie

1876

Beginning of the friendship between the Monet and Hoschedé familie First visit to Montgeron.

1877

Death of Courbet. Spends part of the summer at Montgeron. Erne Hoschedé's ruin.

1878

Auction sale of the Hoschedés' properties. The Hoschedé family join the Monets at Vetheuil. Birth of Michel Monet.

1879

Death of Camille Monet. Alice Hoschedé takes charge of the eight childre (two Monets and six Hoschedés).

1880

Series of The Break-up of the Ice at Vétheuil. Decides for the last time t submit paintings to the Salon. Trip to the Normandy coast.

1881

Trip to the Normandy coast, including visit to his brother Leon i Pétites-Dalles. Painting expedition to Dieppe. Moves to Poissy.

1882

Poissy. Trips to Pourville and surroundings.

1883

Painting expeditions to Le Havre and Etretat. March: one-man show a Durand-Ruel's. Settles at Giverny with Alice Hoschedé and the childre Winter: trip to the Midi and the Italian Riviera with Renoir. Visi Cézanne.

1884

Painting expedition to the Riviera: Bordighera and Menton. Exhibits a Georges Petit's galleries for the Exposition Internationale.

1885

Exhibits at Georges Petit's. Visits Etretat.

1886

Exhibits at Georges Petit's. Disapproves of Durand-Ruel's Impressionis exhibition in New York. Paints in Holland. Shows with the Groupe de Vingt in Brussels.

1887

Paints at Belle-Isle-en-Mer in Brittany, where he meets Gustav Geffroy art critic for Clemenceau's journal La Justice. Re-establishes close friend ship with Clemenceau. Visits Octave Mirbeau at Noirmoutiers.

1888

Disagreement with Durand-Ruel who opens a gallery in New York Signs a contract with Boussod and Valadon. Paints in the Midi.

1889

Successful exhibition with Rodin at Georges Petit's. Paints in centra France. Organises private subscription to purchase Manet's Olympia fo the Louvre. Breaks his contract with Boussod and Valadon.

1889–90

Continues work on series of Haystacks. Buys house in Giverny. End disagreement with Durand-Ruel.

1
hibits the series of *Haystacks* at Durand-Ruel's in Paris. Visits London. ath of Ernest Hoschedé.

2
ntinues work on his studies of Rouen cathedral. Exhibits series of *lars* at Durand-Ruel's in Paris. July 16th: marries Alice Hoschedé.

3
ys the pond at Giverny. Dreyfus condemned. Deaths of Berthe rissot and Caillebotte. Completes many of his studies of Rouen hedral.

4
ry Cassatt and Cezanne visit Giverny.

5
ints in Norway. Twenty of the series *Rouen Cathedral* among ers exhibited at Durand-Ruel's in Paris. Paints series based on water lilies in the pond at Giverny.

6
nting expedition to Pourville.

7
ies of *Rouen Cathedral* exhibited in Venice.

8
ath of Stephane Mallarmé.

9
ath of Sisley. Works on the *Nymphéas*.

0
orks on the *Thames* series in London. New series at Vétheuil.

1
nts in London and Vétheuil. Decides to expand his water lily pond.

2
hibits at the Bernheims' gallery. Works at Giverny on the *Thames* es.

3
ath of Pissarro. Continues working at Giverny on the *Thames* series.

4
hibits *Thames* series at Durand-Ruel's in Paris. Visits the Prado to see works of Velasquez. Paints in London.

5
orks on a new *Thames* series with the aim of several exhibitions in ndon.

6
ath of Cézanne.

8
st painting journey to Venice. First serious trouble with sight.

9
hibits the series of the *Nymphéas*. Alice Monet ill.

0
w and final alterations to the lily pond.

1911
Death of Alice Monet in May. At end of year Monet resumes work and wants to complete series on *Venice*.

1912
Exhibits *Venice* series at the Bernheims' galleries. Meets Pierre Bonnard.

1913
Trip to Switzerland.

1914
Death of Jean Monet. Beginning of First World War. Decides to construct third studio of large dimensions to enable him to work on new series of *Nymphéas*, painted on uncommonly large canvases. Among the many works completed in this studio was *Les Decorations des Nymphéas* (completed only a few months before his death), consisting of nineteen panels, which he presented to the State.

1916
Inauguration of the third studio by Academy Goncourt.

1917
Deaths of Mirbeau, Rodin and Degas.

1919
Death of Renoir.

1921
Sight deteriorates. Experiences great difficulty working on the *Decorations des Nymphéas*.

1922
Death of Paul Durand-Ruel. Double cataract diagnosed. Signs bequest of *Decorations des Nymphéas* in Vernon.

1923
Operation for cataract on the right eye. Able to resume work by the end of the year.

1926
Death of Gustave Geffroy. December 5th: Death of Monet.

Bibliography

Jean-Pierre Hoschedé   Claude Monet ce mal connu
                           Cailler Editeur Genève 196c

Alice Monet   Journal 1863–1910
                           Archives Toulgouat-Piguet

Blanche Monet   Notes sur Claude Monet
                           Archives Toulgouat-Piguet

Pierre Raingo-Pelouse   Généalogie de la famille Raingo

Gustave Geffroy   Claude Monet sa vie son œuvre
                           G. Crès & Cie 1924

Lionello Venturi   Les Archives de l'Impressionnisme
                           Durand-Ruel Editeurs Paris-New York 1939

John Rewald   The History of Impressionism
                           The Museum of Modern Art, New York

Lilla Cabot Perry   Reminiscences of Claude Monet from 1889 to 1909
                           The American Magazine of Art Volume XVIII March 1927 No. 3

Henri Bang   Extraits de Journal 1895. Traduits du norvégien par Jacques
                           Hoschedé

Pierre Toulgouat   Peintres Américains à Giverny
                           Rapports France-Etats-Unis No. 62 mai 1952

Abbé Anatole   Flore de Vernon et de La Roche-Guyon
Toussaint &   *Rouen Julien Lecerf 1898*
Jean-Pierre Hoschedé

Georges Truffaut   Le Jardin de Claude Monet
                           "Jardinage" novembre 1924 No. 87

Félix Breuil   Les iris aux bords des eaux
                           "Jardinage" octobre 1913 No. 21

Albert Le Gal   Journal 1910–1916